T0148052

Let's Do It Again

Let's Do It Again

RICHARD (DIGGER) T. VOGT

authorHOUSE®

AuthorHouse™ LLC
1663 Liberty Drive
Bloomington, IN 47403
www.authorhouse.com
Phone: 1-800-839-8640

© 2014 Richard (Digger) T. Vogt. All rights reserved.

No part of this book may be reproduced, stored in a retrieval system, or
transmitted by any means without the written permission of the author.

Published by AuthorHouse   02/19/2014

ISBN: 978-1-4918-5857-8 (sc)
ISBN: 978-1-4918-5855-4 (hc)
ISBN: 978-1-4918-5854-7 (e)

Library of Congress Control Number: 2014901975

Any people depicted in stock imagery provided by Thinkstock are models,
and such images are being used for illustrative purposes only.
Certain stock imagery © Thinkstock.

This book is printed on acid-free paper.

Because of the dynamic nature of the Internet, any web addresses or links contained in
this book may have changed since publication and may no longer be valid. The views
expressed in this work are solely those of the author and do not necessarily reflect the
views of the publisher, and the publisher hereby disclaims any responsibility for them.

Contents

THIS BOOK IS DEDICATED TO

MISS EUNICE STEEL

WHO TAUGHT ME HOW TO PAINT WITH WORDS

ACKNOWLEDGEMENT

I want to give a special thank you to my loving wife Marlene for her tireless editing of my manuscript and for encouraging me to continue when I was running short on ideas and enthusiasm. She never complained when I was pounding the keyboard and she sat watching a movie all by herself, Her daring pushed me to give the reader something beyond the ordinary.

1—FINKTOWN

December 10, 2013

I was born and raised in a small city that was located along the banks of the Hudson River in upstate New York, about fifty miles north of New York City. I lived in a section of the city known as Finktown. It was so named for a resident of Peekskill who saw potential in the area and bought a few lots in the mid nineteenth century which he sold at a nice profit. The area developed and became known as "Fink's Town". It was located on the periphery of the city and encompassed an area of about ten blocks, much of which was not developed.

I remember Finktown as a place that typified what America stood for. The residents were mostly European immigrants hoping to get a piece of the American pie. They were Italians, Germans, Jews, Portuguese, Blacks, British, French and many more that I just can't recall. Most couldn't write their name in English or speak it very well, but communication wasn't a problem. Many gestures and words are understood universally. They were hard working people who had found their hole in the fence and were determined to create a new world for themselves in the U.S.A.

Finktown abounded in characters, from "the candy man" who dressed to the nines in a derby hat, suit, and overcoat with a velvet collar and gave pieces of candy to any kid who crossed his path. There was Danny Smith, an old black guy who was inebriated most of the time and would dance a little soft shoe routine whenever he was asked. We had "Shoemake," a really old Italian man with his little dog Ruffee. He would grab the hair on the nape of the neck of any kid who ventured too close to him, give it a tug and then giggle. We all took pains to avoid him at all costs. Tommy Boy DiDinato while retarded, played right along with the rest of us. He could bend his fingers back to touch his wrist. Amazing! There were many tough guys in the neighborhood who would fight at the drop of a hat.

Author

Grocery stores were plentiful. Nicolina's grocery on the corner of Lincoln Terrace and Grant Avenue where cigarettes were available for a penny apiece for the teenagers ready to move up to the big time. Bruno's grocery right up the street where we would try to get in the store and out with a pack of cupcakes before they could react to the buzzer located in the back room where they sat and waited for customers. Charles De Revere had a store on Main Street where I got my introduction to gambling. He had a slot type machine in the store that accepted pennies in the slot where they would bounce around metal pegs on the way to the bottom. If one of the center slots stopped the penny, that was a win. If the penny dropped to the bottom, out of luck son! Carmine and Jimmy Verderosa had stores side by side on Main Street and I never could figure that one out. The Royal Scarlet store on Main Street was well stocked and part of a chain. My father had a store in our basement in the nineteen twenty's.

Elmer Pataki (the Governors uncle) used to peddle fruits and vegetables grown on the family farm from a horse and wagon There was a man with a pushcart who would buy old rags. We would put a few bricks in with the rags, but he always caught us. He eventually moved up to a horse and wagon. (capitalist!) Charlie Ingersoll would bring his team of horses pulling a wagon down Lincoln Terrace and we would always try to hitch a ride, but Charlie was pretty quick with that long blacksnake whip he always carried and one crack would quickly dislodge us. The iceman would sometimes chop us a sliver of ice on those hot summer days, and it was really a treat to us. There were vendors selling olive oil by the gallon and spagetti by the case to the Italian families, along with a repairman who caried a manually operated grinding wheel on his back who would sharpen knives and fix umbrellas. There was always the man with the forlorn looking Shetland pony and a camera ready to snap a picture of your sweet little cherub sitting astride his magnificent beast.

We had Penelope Park where we would sit on the stone wall and watch a ball game one day and the next day we would go one of the many carnivals that performed there. The carnivals always had those hootchy kootchy girls as one of the attractions, and as a young boy I usually fell in love with one of them when they performed under the midway lights at night. I saw the same girl down at De Revere's store the next day, and bam!, My love affair was over. Daylight can be be cruel. The carnivals usually had a "geek" who would be placed in a makeshift pit where he would kill a live chicken and chew on it. He was probably some poor old alcoholic who was at the end of his road. Up the street, Penelope Pond gave us unending pleasure with swimming in the summer and ice skating in the winter. The pond was rustic but we all enjoyed the many hours we spent there. It had a float in the center of it and also a diving board. A very basic chlorination system consisted of a steel barrel mounted on a platform which was placed over the brook that fed the pond and a spigot released a drop of the chemical at timed intervals and that was it. The pond had an abundance of frogs, snakes and fish which I'm sure helped keep the water in natural balance.

There was a small factory located on Park Street next to Penelope Pond that manufactured costume jewelry and employed some of the women from the immediate area. Penelope Pond drained into a brook that ran in back of the factory where the women used to toss their mistakes out the windows and into the brook. If a piece didn't measure up to management standards, it was relegated to a watery grave. We would roll up our pantlegs and walk the brook, looking for the gem like pieces of glass. There were always bracelets and rings to be found, slightly defective, but never the less they always impressed the local damsels when they reluctantly accepted them. Salvaged gifts from what the local people always referred to as the "Pearl Factory".

There were nicknames galore in Finktown. Names like Jumbo, Steamboat, Meatball Marks, Ducky, Shocky Weinger, Dirty Dan, Wumpy, Scootch, Chickenhead, Dip Depew, Beansie Vogt Blackie Miozzi and many more. Girls were never given nick names. I guess we must have held them in high regard in those days.

There were the forty thieves who had a sign nailed over the top of their clubhouse door that read "we steal anything that isn't nailed down". Ahhh yes, the Robin Hoods of Finktown! Their club house was down on Grant Avenue on a lot that also had an empty house on it that the old timers in the neighborhood called ":the madhouse". I never knew why they referred to it that way. On this same lot, there would be visits by traveling medicine shows where they would have Indians on stage to gather a crowd so that the glib tongued hawkers could foist their elixirs on the public. Elixirs that they guaranteed would cure anything from flat feet to a ruptured appendix. People flocked to these shows and bought this alcohol tinged liquid with the hope of everlasting life on earth but all they ever got was a cheap drunk!

Donny Gerow had a bar/diner on the corner of Armstrong Avenue and Main where a guy could get drunk on the beer and sober up on the coffee in one afternoon. Fried egg on a hard roll was high on the food chain for the Finktown Boys. Abie Etner had the Peekskill Bottling Works on Main Street where I was employed one summer. The Osborne Studebaker dealership was located next door. It was a classy car that eventually became a collector item after they stopped manufacturing them. Music from the black church adjacent to Park Street School would thunder forth on Sunday mornings with everyone in attendance adorned in their finest attire. There was the Peekskill CIty Laundry where I once tried to get a job and was relieved when I didn't get hired after the manager gave me a tour of the hot steamy interior. I couldn't figure out how the old ladies that were employed there could survive the workplace conditions. (air conditioning was not yet available)

We didn't need television or video games for entertainment in Finktown, the neighborhood provided all the fun we needed. There were always a lot of people on the street. Parents calling for their brood, girls skipping rope or playing hop scotch, boys playing a game of baseball in the street or just rollerskating. There was always a gang hanging around the corner waiting for some kid to show up with a nickel so they could share in a Drakes Cake or get a swig of soda. The smells of Italian cooking filled the air with the fragrance of oregano and fennel at suppertime while the aroma of grapes being readied for wine making produced a bouquet reminiscent of the Napa Valley. We never went hungry in Finktown, just about everyone had a garden and the fruits and vegetables were ours for the taking. Cherry trees, apple trees, pear trees and grape vines were all within our reach, but we had to be quick. We took just enough for the moment and I'm sure that whatever we took was never missed.

Finktown is gone now, but it will always remain in the hearts of he people who lived there, those who ate a piece of candy from the candy man or who witnessed Danny doing the soft shoe. Yes, the buildings are still there, many of the trees are still growing and the streets are the same. But it was the people who made Finktown the unforgettable place that it was. It was a once in a lifetime experience that I and many others had the pleasure of enjoying and one of the most memorable times of my life.

Richard T Vogt

2—WINTERING IN FINKTOWN

March 20, 2009

The smell of burning leaves, withered cornstalks and tomato plants in the gardens, and barrels of sand being placed on all the steep hills in the neighborhood; getting ready for winter in Fink-town.

The smell of burning leaves permeated the air almost every day. Kids and grownups all joined in the fun. If some housewife had her wash out on the line, she would inform the pyromaniac in no uncertain terms to extinguish the fire. Most of the burning took place in the gutters of the road. There were blackened gutters all over Finktown. Kids would make huge piles of leaves in their yards and jump in them for hours. We didn't worry about ticks back then.

Life was quite different in the winter than the summer. Getting prepared for and enduring those cold winter months took a lot of doing and a big change in routine for most of the residents. The ice man didn't make his daily trips to sell that twenty five or fifty cent piece of ice. Most people just placed their perishables out in the elements to keep them from spoiling. In our house, we just moved the whole ice box out on the back porch or "back stoop" as my father referred to it. A "stoop" was a little smaller than a porch. When the ice man did deliver a piece of ice to a house, he didn't have any way to accurately measure the piece really, he would just poke the ice pick in where he figured it should go and lopped off a piece. Usually some irate housewife could be heard complaining loudly that she got an undersized piece much to the chagrin of the ice man. On a real hot day, he would give us chips of ice which we considered a real treat.

Winter was the time that the coal man came visiting. His appearance didn't leave any doubt in anyone's mind just what his occupation was.

He was usually covered from head to toe with black coal dust. Coal men always seemed to have pearly white teeth. The unusual feature of the coal that we burned in our stoves and furnaces was that it gave of a blue flame. I mean so what, heat is heat. But the distributors of the coal really highlighted that blue flame. We had a room in the cellar of the house where the coal was stored and the coal man would either carry his load in a canvas bag or if he could get the truck up in the driveway, chute it in to the "coal bin" right from the truck. It was dirty, tough, hard work done by tough hard men. If kids were not well behaved around Christmas time, they were threatened with coal in their stocking if their behavior didn't improve, and believe it or not, it usually worked.

Coal supplied what heat we had with an occasional kerosene stove added here and there in some homes. Most houses had a central furnace and a cook stove in the kitchen. When we went to bed, my father would bank the furnace, that is to slow the rate of burn so that there was hardly any heat coming from the central register. I mean man, it was cold in the bedrooms. I was visiting my cousin one day and when we were in his bedroom, I saw a glass of water on his dresser that was frozen solid. The sleeping arrangements called for three in a bed in large families like mine. There were nine kids in a house of about eleven hundred square feet in size. We would throw anything on the bed that would provide warmth, and the dog was always welcome. When we got up in the morning, we all headed for that hot air register that was now providing heat, thanks to my father for opening the damper. The register grate got so hot, it would burn our feet. My father finally splurged and bought a two burner kerosene stove and put it in the upstairs bedrooms. We were warmer but now everything we wore smelled like kerosene including us. I don't know why we weren't put to sleep permanently due to the lack of oxygen in the rooms because I dont believe the stove was vented.

To supplement our coal supply, my father used to take a burlap bag and go to the Villa Loretta to pick "coke" from the slag pile to burn in our furnace. Coke was a byproduct of the soft coal that they burned in their furnaces. Finktowners always referred to the school as the "Sisters" because it was operated by the nuns of the Catholic church.

It was not uncommon for girls to escape from the school and be found hiding in someone's back yard. As kids, the place held a facination for us and we would frequently wander over on to the property only to be chased by the nuns. We were scared to death of them because we had never before seen anything like the sisters of the church their habits.

Kindling wood was needed to start the fires in the house and a good source for the kindling was the grocery stores in the business section of the city. Oranges, lettuce and such were transported in wooden slatted boxes which were discarded after they were emptied. My father would pay me five cents for every box I brought home, and I would go downtown very early in the morning and pile them on my wagon or sled and haul them home. Sometimes, when pickings were scarce, fights would break out for salvage rights among the boys who were scavenging for boxes. I tried to avoid that, but if I couldn't, I had four older brothers that would avenge any bruises I picked up there.

All the burning of coal in the homes resulted in barrels of ashes to be disposed of, but first the ashes had to be sifted to to salvage the unburned "Klinkers" which could be burned agan. The klinkers were just chunks of coal that didn't burn the first time around. The ashes were shoveled into a makeshift screen box and shaken vigoriously which would leave the large pieces in the box. Those pieces were the "Klinkers" The ash residue would be saved to sprinkle on the sidewalk to provide traction for the pedestrians.

When an ice storm hit the area, getting down off the hill with a car was a challenge. One time, after a ferocious storm, I backed out of the driveway not knowing how slick it was and my car went careening down the sidewalk and crashed into a large sand barrel. I had to hire a tow truck to get my car to a level sidestreet. The snow and ice storms provided great conditions for sledding down the street I lived on. It was very steep and quite a ride. Some of us used what we called "dummy" sleds which were homemade and not maneuverable due to a lack of any steering apperatus. We would always post a lookout at the cross streets for passing cars and when the clear signal was given, we would bellywop the sled and away we would go. If the lookout yelled "here comes a car" we would dig in our toes on the road and if that didn't stop us we abandoned ship. Most auto owners took their cars off the road for the winter so there really wasn't much traffic. When the city workers would come to sand the hill so the traffic could move up and down, we would get out our shovels and cover the sand in the middle of the road with snow and continue our fun after they left. In those days, there were no mechanical sand spreaders attached to the back of the trucks. A laborer would stand on the sand in the back of the truck and the truck would back slowly up the hill while the laborer threw shovels full of sand on the road as fast as he could. The snow on the sides of the road wasn't carted away in those days, There were huge piles along each roadway and the kids would make forts and igloos to provide protection during the many snowball fights that took place all day long.

Penelope pond was the main source of recreation during the winter months. It was a great place to ice skate and just about everyone in Finktown used to go there. Many would bring along shovels when it snowed and a skating area was cleared in no time. We used to call our attempts to skate "ankle skating" due to the lack of ankle support in the skates. A favorite game to play was "crack the whip" where a long line of hand holding skaters would get moving in a straight line until the desired speed was achieved, then the lead skater would stop short or quickly change direction which would cause all the skaters to tumble onto one another. Great fun! A huge bonfire was always roaring on the bank of the pond with a never ending supply of firewood obtained from a vacant house across the street. It was a great place for matchmaking.

Listening to the radio was the main form of entertainment during the winter months with an occasional movie at the Paramount theatre when it was affordable. The price of admission was just eleven cents. The weekly radio shows were The Shadow Knows with Lamont Cranston, Gang Busters, Lux presents Hollywood, Jack Benny, Amos'n Andy, Gillete cavalcade of sports (with Don Dumphy counting for the knockdown at the bell), Fred Allen and many more providing hours of pleasure as we all crowded around the Atwater Kent radio on those cold winter nights and went to those far away places in our minds.

My father always bought baby chicks as winter was nearing it's end and raised them to sell in the neighborhood. He would house them in a coop in the back yard and had a kerosene stove in the coop to keep the little buggers warm. On a Palm sunday morning the stove must have malfunctioned in some way and the coop burned down with all the chicks inside. It was a sad day to say the least.

The next Sunday, (Easter Sunday) the lady who owned the corner grocery store called me and my sister down and presented us with two dyed baby chicks each in colorful boxes. Gestures like that were what made Finktown such a great place to live.

Nothing was wasted in Finktown homes, times were tough and we had to survive as best we could. I remember that we used to get oleo in one pound square bricks and it was pure white. A cellophane packet of powdered dye was included in the box. The dye was sprinkled on the oleo and mixed into it with a fork until the oleo was yellow. Now we had quasi butter. I remember one time when my dad was painting the kitchen we lost the dye packet and had to eat white oleo. It was like spreading lard on the bread. If that wasn't bad enough, the paint my father used contained lead and that lead got into the oleo stored in the icebox. We ate lead flavored white oleo. Waste not, want not!.

Yes, wintering in Finktown required a certain amount of tenacity and a lot of covers on the bed, but we always survived and had a lot of fun taking on the elements that mother nature thrust upon us. Does anyone remember toe punk? What the heck was that? I look back and wonder what the kids of today would have thought of the Finktown of old. Would they have been able to cope? Would they have had as much fun as we did? For we certainly had loads of fun coming through the years. I'll never know, but I will always remember and cherish the good old days there and my memories of "wintering in Finktown" will stay with me forever.

Richard T Vogt

3—DAINS FARM

January 9, 2009

When reminiscing about my youthful days in Finktown, I would be remiss if I didn't mention the role that Dains farm and Skip, the foremen, played in the life of many Finktown boys.

Dains Farm was located just beyond the boundary of the city limits and encompassed about twenty five acres. Most of the young boys in Finktown spent some portion of their adolescent years working around the farm. The foreman of the farm was Skip Morro but most of us referred to him as Skip Dain. Just a quirk of youthful exuberance I guess. His real name was Lawrence and the only person to call him that was Mrs. Dain. The older, bolder boys sometimes called him "Baldy" which he was. He ran the farm with an iron hand, and it was either work or v.t.p.i. (vacate the premises immediately). When there was absolutely nothing left to do among the many necessary chores on the farm, it was time to pick up a pair of grass shears which we referred to as "dew clippers" and start trimming the grass anywhere it needed attention. It was a job most of us despised.

The farm was owned by a wealthy family who operated a few lumber yards in the area. They lived in what we called the "big house" and we rarely saw them or came in contact with them. The entire farm was meticulously groomed and the buildings were maintained like a show place. I once saw the owner when she came down to the barn to give some specific instructions to the foreman. I remember she drove a late thirties or early forties Lincoln Zephyr and it was an impressive automobile.

To work for a time on the farm was sort of a rite of passage for most of the kids I grew up with. It served as an apprenticeship for going out in the cruel world to make a living. It was an enjoyable place to be and we performed the chores willingly and always tried to do our best. The chores taught us responsibility and aided us in using the decision making process in our early years. Skip was a good mentor and gave us jobs to do that required independent action and that was essential in our formative years. We didn't receive any compensation for the work we did other than the satisfaction of being there, working with the animals and enjoying the camaraderie of each other. I should mention that we had an initiation ritual for any newcomers to join the ranks on the farm. After the newbie got acclimated to the routine and felt comfortable with the rest of us, we would lure him into the cow barn and once we got him there, we would all pounce on him. We then lowered his trousers and smeared a heavy glob of cow manure in an unmentionable spot. Most took it good naturedly and looked forward to the day when a newcomer would walk into the barnyard.

All the heavy labor on the farm was done with a draft horse named "Bunk". He lived to the ripe old age of twenty nine years. I don't believe I have ever seen a more gentle animal than Bunk. When we would unhook him from the harness after a day of work, two or three of us would get on his back and ride him from the barnyard up to the inside of the barn where his stall was located. When he died, the hole which was dug to bury him was to small for his legs as rigor mortise had set in. My brother Jimmy ran up, got a saw, and lopped his legs off. Now it was a good fit. But I often wondered how old bunk got around up there in horse heaven. His replacement was another draft horse six years of age named Harry. Now he was a piece of work. To say Harry was spirited was like saying iced tea in Georgia is a little sweet. He would really feel his oats on those cool mornings and sometimes would just take off for no reason when we had him hitched to the wagon and then we would have a job retrieving him. There was a piece of equipment used on the farm called a "stone boat" which was made of oak timbers about six inches square. It was flat and about twelve by five feet with the front raised up like the prow of a ship. It was used to clear the fields of large stones by rolling them onto the flat surface of the stone boat. Those stones made the many walls that are found in the middle of nowhere. We would hook Harry up to the boat in the early morning when the dew was still on the tall grass in the fields and go down and slide that stone boat all over the place. We had a lot of fun doing that and we always did it on the sly. But looking back now, I'm sure skip was on to us and just let a few young boys have some fun. He was a great guy.

The farm had a huge vegetable garden which we were expected to keep weed free. There was even an asparagus bed which would go to seed at the end of its maturity with shoots about six feet high. I remember the huge multicolored spiders that used to lounge on the plants. Skip grew all the garden plants from seeds in the green house located on the property down below the barnyard. On a warm day, the air in the greenhouse was stifling. Skip probably gave away as many plants as he used for the garden. Occasionally I would find a parsnip in the garden and I would take it home to have my mother fry it for me. To a Finktown kid, that was a delicacy, believe me. The garden always flourished with the application of manure that was in never ending supply from the livestock.

The farm had three milking cows and an occasional calf, pigs, chickens, geese and many many cats. Whenever anyone's cat in the neighborhood had kittens that couldn't be adopted out to a neighbor, they were usually shunted off to the farm. It was amusing to see Skip shoot a stream of warm milk into a cats mouth when he was milking the cows. As you can imagine, there were very few rats around the place. The cow barn had an aroma that I remember to this day, there was nothing like it. On a cold winter day when the cows weren't turned out in the pasture to graze, it was always toasty warm in the barn. I was always amazed how the cows went to their own yoke in the barn when we bought them in from the pasture at night. I still remember the slaughter of a steer that was raised on the farm. As young kids, we looked at him as a pet, like a dog or cat, but on a farm, a steer is strictly beef on the hoof. They led him to the barnyard, then struck him on the forehead with a sledge hammer and slit his throat. It is probably one of the reasons that I am a vegetarian today. But I realize that it was simply the way of farm life.

I was often given the job of collecting the eggs. I would frequently find a double yolk egg and Skip would let me take it home. I remember being extra careful on the way home with that egg, cupping it in my hand like some precious jewel. It was special to be given something like that. It wouldn't mean a thing to a boy of today, such are the times. Occasionally a hen would get the urge to sit on her eggs to hatch them. We would put her in a box about four feet square with a hinged lid on it for a couple of days and she would lose the desire to sit on the eggs.

Haying time meant a lot of hustle for everyone involved. The cooperation of the weather was essential when getting in the hay. If it rained after it was cut, the crop was ruined. Cutting and raking the hay was done with horse drawn equipment. A sickle bar for cutting and a rake equipped with a foot operated lever to raise the rake to form rows. After the sun dried it out it was tossed onto a flat wagon with pitchforks and taken to the barn where it was thrown up into the hay loft. It was tough labor intensive work. One day my brother got stabbed through the arm with a pitch-fork. Mrs Dain took him to the doctor to be sewn up and then to our house to notify my parents. My brother rode back to the farm with her to continue haying. (lawsuit? what the heck is that)?

The hayloft was a pleasant place to be with the sweet aroma of the dried hay providing a treat for the sense of smell. It had a chute which went from the loft to the cow barn two floors below. The hay was dropped down the chute and the cows had their dinner. The wood timbers on the side of the chute were polished to a high finish from all the years of use. We would get roughhousing up in the hay loft and invariably one of us would get shoved down the chute, but. there was always a big pile of hay there to break our fall.

The farm had two apple orchards located on opposite sides of the property. I dont know what they did with all the apples because there had to be many bushels produced by both orchards. The property had a swimming pool that appeared to be non-functioning for may years. It was at one time filled by the brook that ran through the property but was now just a foul smelling mess. It was at one time a pretty fancy pool with metal posts spaced at intervals around the perimeter and cherub statues providing a serene setting. Alongside the pool, there was a wall that supported the roadway up to the barn. There was a root cellar built into the wall and I can still recall going in there and being overcome by the dark, dank, mustiness of the place. In the hottest summer day, it was always cold in there.

Most kids in my time didn't have much to hang around the house for, so in effect, the farm sort of became a home away from home. There was always a group of our peers there and bad behavior wasn't tolerated. Theft was nonexistent because theft on anyone's part meant banishment from the farm forever, and no kid wanted that. We all learned a lot there. Skip would give us a chore to do that required independent decision making and the ability to work cohesively with a group. We were all gaining knowledge during our apprenticeship that we would use later in our adult lives. I don't know how many years the farm was a haven for the Finktown boys, but it wasn't long enough. I think that most of the boys who spent time there would agree it was an unforgettable experience in their life and that Skip was a great guy. Unfortunately, most of us don't realize that until time has passed and we look back. But such is life.

I remember that on December 7th 1941 I came home from the farm and my mother informed me that the Japanese had attacked Pearl Harbor. Many of the older Finktown boys went into the service and in a few years, the crowd dwindled at the farm. Then the ownership of the farm changed and the new owner made it known that he didn't want a bunch of Finktown boys cluttering up the place. I'm sure Skip missed us and we certainly missed his guidance and friendship. Many of the boys went up to visit when they were home on leave and i'm sure Skip appreciated that.

I reminisce quite often about the good times on the farm and I'm sure my wife is tired of hearing the stories about the place. But the good tmes in our lives seem to stick to us like some sort of adhesive and it's hard to let go. I hope that whoever reads these ramblings gets some enjoyment out of them and it leaves them with a feel for what life was like in the old days in Finktown.

Richard T Vogt

4—FINKTOWN GOES TO WAR

March 30, 2009

December 7th 1941, the Imperial Japanese Navy launched a surprise attack on the U. S. naval base in Pearl Harbor and the majority of the U. S. naval fleet was in ruins while at anchor. "A day that will live in infamy" declared the president of the United States, Franklin Delano Roosevelt. The country was angry, the country vowed revenge, and Finktown went to war!!!!!

I returned from a day at Dains farm on a sunday afternoon and my mother informed me of the cowardly attack by the Japanese in Pearl Harbor, Hawaii. I was only nine years old at the time and it really didn't mean that much to me as I remember. Little did I know the impact that the coming war would have on me and my family. All the young men of Finktown knew what was coming. It was only a matter of time when those boys of draft-able age would be called by their Uncle Sammy to put down their pool cues and pick up a rifle. They were going to be soldiers! Many of them didn't wait to be drafted, they went down and enlisted in the various branches of the military. The war really put a dent in the pool of eligible bachelors in Finktown. Those who were drafted ended up in the army and the boys who enlisted usually opted for the Navy. A few brave souls went into the U. S. Marines. There was an abundance of going away parties being held in the neighborhood for the next year. Some were married men with children and were called into duty alongside the single men. (Uncle Sam was an equal opportunity employer)!! There were only a few families in the neighborhood that didn't have to give up one or more of their boys to the war effort. Our household offered three of my brothers to the cause. Most of the boys who went into the service had never even left home before, so it was a significant event in not only their lives but in the lives of their loved ones.

Finktown immediately went int the defense mode. Homeowners were notified of new wartime regulations that affected all of the residents. Blackout shades, air raid drills, (I can still hear the warden shouting "get those lights out") during a nighttime air raid drill. Car headlights had to be painted black halfway down from the top of the lens. Rationing of just about every commodity available to the public went into effect. Gas stamps were issued to those fortunate enough to own a car, and Items like sugar, and meat could only be purchased in amounts compatible with the value of ones food stamps.

And as a blow to the fairer sex, nylon stockings were almost impossible to buy. Women resorted to painting the stocking seams on their bare legs (yes, there were seams on the stockings in the old days). Hooray, no more runs! I remember my uncle coming up from Brooklyn with a case of condensed milk for us and that was like manna from heaven. We could lighten and sweeten our coffee in one application., Now that was something. He lived in the section of Brooklyn that was controlled by the Gallo brothers so I'm sure there was always a lot of contraband available there.

Gasoline was hard to come by unless you knew where the black market gas was being sold. If a driver was willing to part with some green, it was readily available. like almost everything else, stamps were issued to automobile owners according to their needs and still, amounts were limited. Most people didn't keep their cars on the road and those who did had many ways to conserve fuel. They would shut the engine off and coast down the inclines, and just slow down when the were picking someone up so they could jump on the running board while the car was in motion. Some people mixed kerosene with their gas and wow, they produced some heavy duty smoke. Cars had a distinctive smell in those days, and whenever I catch a whiff of that smell to this day, it takes me back.

Coal and kerosene were scarce and expensive which forced many homeowners to burn wood. I remember a neighbor who had a rig in his backyard to saw logs. It was a thirty inch diameter steel blade with sharp teeth, mounted on a shaft which was powered by a 1932 Dodge engine. No car body, just the chassis and the drive train. A large belt was wrapped around a rear tire and then was connected to the saw blade shaft. That contraption would really whine when it was cutting through a log. Start the Dodge, throw it in gear, and you were ready to saw some wood. When not in use, a half of a car tire was placed over the saw blade for safety. A dangerous set up if I ever saw one!

The city fathers thought it would be patriotic if everyone had a garden, so they had a farmer come down to plow up a few acres for "citizen victory gardens". Each applicant was allotted a small portion of the site to grow whatever they chose. I remember one fellow who used to ride up on his bike every day to tend his little patch. Needless to say, Finktowners ate good from the gardens.

Most of us had brothers serving in the war zone and were proud of them. One guy in the neighborhood was in the army and had the misfortune of being stationed at the West Point Military Academy. He was home just about every night and when he drove through the neighborhood, he really got razzed by all of the kids on the corner. I don't know why he didn't take a different route to his house, maybe he never thought of it. One particular night he drove on through and someone yelled "slaaacker". He jammed on the brakes and jumped out of his car and inquired as to who made the remark. One of the bigger boys of about sixteen just walked up to him and defiantly stated "I did". The soldier got back in his car and drove away.

He never passed through the gauntlet again. and the boy who challenged him was our hero. Incidentally, he joined the marines a short time later.

Homes who had given their young men to the war had flags in their windows with the number of stars corresponding to the number of boys serving. My house proudly displayed three stars. A gold star indicated a serviceman killed in action.

There were paper drives constantly as there were scrap metal drives. Aluminum foil was always rolled up into a big ball and donated at the scrap metal drives. Lucky strike cigarettes changed the color of their package from green to red and adopted the slogan "Lucky Strike green has gone to war" Conservation was the rule, don't waste anything.

Support for the boys over there was ever foremost in the minds of all Finktowners. We were taught patriotic songs in grade school and sang them at rally's to promote war bond sales. "Put your shoulder to the wheel, let the foe know how we feel" were words from a favorite song which was written by a local. There wasn't much to be had, but Finktown did put it's shoulder to the wheel.

There was a camp of British Sailors out on main street whose ship had been sunk and they could be seen staggering back to the bivouac at dusk. They weren't given the welcome mat by the local boys, but I do remember that quite a few of the local sweeties made themselves good will ambassadors to Britain. This of course, led to frequent hostile action by some of the local gladiators. The fact that the British sailors were sleeping in tents just made that dour British disposition a little more tart. They didn't stay very long as I recall. I remember convoys of army trucks filled with soldiers rolling down main street and the men throwing fistfuls of letters out of the trucks hoping some patriotic bystander would mail them. Squadrons of bombers would fly over Finktown once in a while and it would draw a big cheer from the crowds on the streets.

Finktown was definitely a more quiet place with all the boys away fighting the war overseas, but thankfully, the war finally ended. There was pandemonium on the streets when the end of the war was announced. There were wild, crazy celebrations being held in every corner of the city and people were ecstatic. When they started coming home, some of the boys changed for the better and some not so. The main thing I remember is that all the Finktown boys got home in one piece. One was captured by the Germans and held for a while, but he too got home eventually. Most of the returning vets signed up for the 52/20 club. It was a government benefit to the veterans that gave them twenty dollars a week for fifty two weeks. (pretty good money back then). Many vets signed on to the G.I. bill to go back to school or start a business venture. I remember a few taking classes when I was in high school. The people of Finktown got on with their lives and everything went back to being what it was before the war.

It was still a place where you could be entertained by the neighborhood while sitting on your front porch. The atmosphere and the characters that roamed the streets and hung out on the corners were back to create that charm that was Finktown.

Richard T Vogt

5—GHOST CAMP

October 15, 2013

Me and four of my buddies were hanging around the corner on a hot Saturday afternoon trying to figure out something different to do to pass the time. We were all about eleven or twelve years old and had a thirst for adventure. We would come up with an idea and it would be quickly replaced by another. Someone mentioned a log cabin we had discovered in a deeply wooded section by a county reservoir that was about ten miles out of town. We had discovered it by accident just roaming around the area a few months ago. At the time, we were told to avoid the place because the landowner didn't take kindly to trespassers. It was completely isolated and the only way to gain entrance to the site was through an old long ago abandoned cemetery. It was in a run down condition and was inhabited only by wild animals that wandered in and out of the place when we discovered it. We decided that this would be our adventure of the summer. We were going camping! It took us about two weeks to gather the equipment we would need for what we figured would be a one week stay in the wilderness. After talking about it and tossing ideas around, we decided to really rough it. Our diet would consist mainly of beans, Dinty Moore stew and Franco American spaghetti.

In addition to the canned staples, we figured we would supplement our canned food diet with fish we would catch from the reservoir and and any wild game we were ingenious enough to snare.

Our equipment would be a few few ratty blankets, canteens for water, fishing line and hooks, a pot and a frying pan. I even planned on sneaking a 22 rifle out of the house for a little added protection. You can already see that this was to be a serious endeavor. None of us had any experience living in the wild with the exception of a few back yard sleep outs in a tent. We figured we would make our bedding with hemlock boughs cut from the trees that were abundant in the area. Matches, we knew that without matches, one could not survive in the woods for long. Its funny, we didn't think of any first aid equipment, Youth tends to disregard any thought of injury of any kind.

When we started planning the trip, the list of campers grew to about eight, but as the days passed, parental intervention and just a loss of nerve whittled it back down to the original five hardy souls. We were the talk of the neighborhood and all the girls looked at us as settlers going off to blaze a new Oregon Trail. It was quite a trek out to the site where the cabin was located so we kept our backpacks light. We were basking in the limelight. California, here we come!!

We all met down at the corner hangout loaded with what we felt would sustain us in the cabin for five days. We were probably a sorry looking sight. We knew there was a spring near the cabin so drinking water wouldn't be a problem. I'm sure each of had mixed feelings about what we were going to do, but the few people that had gathered around us to see us off stifled any feelings we had about withdrawing from the venture at this late date. We fortified ourselves with a healthy breakfast of hostess cupcakes and nehi orange soda and then with little adieu, we were on our way.

We each had our own equipment and split up the provisions we would need so that we all had just about an equal load. As we headed up the street, people standing in their yards or on their porches were calling out words of encouragement and giving advice. One yelled "watch out for Ben, he's crazy". This last remark put a lump in my throat. The owner was known to behave in an eccentric manner to trespassers. We figured that we wouldn't have any problem with him as we we were going to enter his property from the end opposite to where he lived. Still, that lump persisted! We trudged along, reaching the main highway that would take us to the dirt road on which the log cabin was located. We still had a ways to go. A few of us were developing blisters on our feet probably from the ill fitting shoes we were wearing and the socks that had worn away miles back.

We spotted a pick-up truck coming up in back of us and were desperate enough now to start screaming and yelling for a ride. (with nobody around to pat us on the back, the shine was starting to wear off our trip already) The truck belonged to a dairy farmer who had a farm on the road. He stopped and we all piled in on top of boxes full of food waste that were intended for the few pigs that he raised. The stench was sickening. We held our noses until we reached his farm where we hastily departed the rancid truck. As he drove into his farm, his last remark to us was "watch out for Ben, he's crazy". The lump in my throat tightened even more!. We felt that we were on our own now. No way to contact anyone. We headed on down the dirt road looking for the point at which we would vector off and enter the old cemetery which would take us to our destination.

We found the entrance to the cemetery which was marked by a large rock that looked as if it was plucked from the collection at Stonehenge. The markers in the cemetery were just that, Markers. Some had inscriptions on them which were worn away by time so that they were no longer legible. I remember one where we could still read the letters "Little Willie" which was probably the resting place of a small child or a very short man. Some dated as far back as the eighteenth century. One cluster had about six stones all the same size and condition that were lined up in a row which indicated to us that an epidemic of some sort had claimed an entire family or clan. As we carefully wound our way down the steep grade between the stones, we noticed a rather large hole. We decided that it was either a grave that was dug but never filled or maybe grave robbers, who knows?

The descent down the treacherous slope finally ended and right there in front of us was the log cabin. It looked worse than we remembered. One corner had a large hole in the roof and there were no doors or windows. Just openings. As we approached the structure, there was a strong odor of skunk. The interior was strewn with debris left by hunters who had probably slept overnight in their quest to slay the mighty reindeer. We cleared the debris (beer cans) out and made the interior almost suitable for human habitation. It was now late afternoon and we were famished from our long walk so we started a fire and as the old timers used to say "put on the feedbag". We scouted around and found a stand of hemlock trees and started hacking off enough boughs to provide a soft place to sleep on. We tidied the interior up and each of us picked a spot for their bedding. The shadows were growing longer and dusk was rapidly approaching. Soon it would be show time. Alone in the wilderness!

The darkness came on to us quickly as soon as the sun set. We never realized that there is not much to do after dark out in the woods. We were all equipped with flashlights but didn't want to use up the batteries reading. And beside that, what would we read? We started telling stories we had heard from grownups about incidents that had happened to people in isolated situations such as we were, but soon our imaginations ran wild to the point where we stopped and just listened to the silence of the night. All of a sudden we heard what sounded like someone walking in the brush near the cabin. We peered out the open windows but couldn't see anything in the pitch black darkness. The cabin was probably a mile from any other houses so it didn't seem like it was anyone just out for walk. Then, I thought of the warnings we were given, "watch out for Ben, he's crazy". Maybe it was him, and maybe he is crazy, I thought, (The lump in my throat now felt like a grapefruit). I took out the 22 rifle that I had sneaked out of the house and assembled the stock to the barrel. I yelled "we've got a gun and we'll shoot". More rustling came from the brush and I fired a round up in the air. The noise stopped and quiet reigned again.

After that, none of us could sleep. We all just sat there and stared into space. Scenes from all the horror movies we had ever seen were running through our minds and we were wishing we were home. We never realized that the night could be so dark. Throughout the night, our fertile imaginations were conjuring up all kinds of noises, creating ghostly creatures from a moonbeam casting a shadow on the log wall and generally convincing us that we were not cut out to be mountain men. We all decided right there that we would have to swallow our pride and hightail it for home at first light.

At the crack of dawn, we packed our belongings and headed up the slope to the road where we hoped to find the farmer ready for a run to town for his pig slop. We were able to hitch a ride with the farmer and got home about ten in the morning. I had no regrets, we tried it and found we couldn't do it, But at least we tried. We took some razzing from the other kids but I'm sure that those that didn't go with us inwardly wished they did. To try and fail is no disgrace but to never try makes the heart a lonely hunter!

Richard T Vogt

6—MY FIRST CAR

October 6, 2013

My first car! Now that was a day of all days. Goodby bicycle, hello speedy travel. I will never forget my first automobile, It was a 1936 ford custom two door sedan. Its hard to convey how I felt when I got behind the wheel for the first time. Point A to point B in a flash. I was literally the king of the road. The car had a ford flat head V8 engine that developed 85 horsepower. Now that was a lot of horsepower in those days. I bought the car in 1949 and paid One hundred fifty dollars for it. It was very special to me because I earned the money used to purchase the vehicle. That was the last time I paid cash for a car for quite a few years. After that, it was as little as possible down and monthly payments that stretched out like telephone poles on a long Texas highway.

I bought it from the father of a girl who I knew quite well and had ridden in it many time so I knew It was in excellent condition. In fact, about six months before I purchased it, a fire erupted in the engine compartment and the wiring had all been replaced after the engine was cleaned. The body was painted midnight blue and the paint was flawless. If the car had any drawbacks, it would have to be that it was equipped with mechanical brakes. When pressure was applied to the brake pedal, that pressure was transmitted to the brakes by a metal cable. This cable over time tended to stretch and that meant less pressure applied to the brakes. In that case, I would have to crawl under the car and tighten a turnbuckle (simply a threaded bolt) to increase the tension on the cables. I had to do this quite often. I would get in heavy bumper to bumper traffic and then be unable to stop short which would result in my smashing into the car in front of me. Fortunately all cars in those days were equipped with heavy metal bumpers so the lack of good brakes didn't really present much of a problem.

I now was one of the few guys in high school to have my own transportation. There were about a dozen or so students that had transportation of their own so naturally we were envied by most of the other guys. There was one student whose father owned the local Chevy dealership who always wheeled around in a nicer car than the principal.

I was a back yard mechanic in those days. I performed all the minor maintenance work on my car such as changing oil, mufflers, spark plugs and considered myself a threat to Carrol Shelby.

And there was plenty to do. In those days, cars weren't as reliable as todays vehicles. The work was messy and done with a minimum of necessary tools. If you were fortunate enough to have a buddy working part time in a garage, you had hit pay dirt. You could usually perform your work there at off hours when the boss wasn't around.

When I enlisted in the navy during the Korean war, I gave the car to my brother in law to use while I was gone. I soon came home for a weekend when a few of us were whooping it up one night and someone got the Idea to go to a dance club in a neighboring town about fifteen miles up river. About five of us jumped in the ford and headed north.

We were just about there when a tire blew. Well, with no way to contact anyone for help, I decided to ride it in on the flat tire. By the time we got to our destination, the tire was severely shredded and the tire rim was ruined. I parked the ford in front of the joint and we went inside and stayed till closing. I decided that I would leave the car there and pick it up next weekend when I knew I would be home on liberty. We called a friend to pick us up at two in the morning and he arrived about an hour later driving a nineteen forty eight Dodge business coupe and was carrying two passengers with him. A business coupe was a Dodge model designed for salesman and usually driven by salesman because it had a very large trunk to carry their wares securely.

The very large trunk naturally meant a very small back seat, which meant we were in for a very cramped ride home. It really wasn't that uncomfortable considering we had two girls with us who were very well endowed.

When I got home the following week-end, I couldn't find my car. I went to the local police and was told that the mayor had my car towed as it was overparked(whatever that means) I located the garage where it was stored and was informed that I not only would have to purchase a tire, tube, and rim, but also pay storage fees for a week while the car was parked in an open field. The man certainly wasn't a believer in "support our troops". We all piled in and the Blue Streak was back on the road.

There was a stock car track at the lower end of town where we would go to watch the maniacs create blood chilling collisions on Saturday nights. The drivers used nineteen thirty seven through nineteen forty Fords which they had laboriously overhauled to obtain maximum speed and minimum braking ability. There were no mufflers and they really roared. Naturally when the races were over, I wanted to get that sound from my car. I climbed under my beauty and punched a few holes in the muffler and now I was Barney Oldfield. VaaaRoooom! Well, that sound lasted a few weeks until the local police convinced me to attach some noise suppression to my vehicle. Now, changing a muffler wasn't an easy task using hand tools. First the car was driven up on cement blocks so I had room to work a hammer and chisel to peel the old muffler off. Then came the rust shower all over my head from splitting the muffler collar off the tailpipe. (sometimes this could be avoided by wrapping an asbestos sheet around the muffler, covering it with a sheet of tin and tightening two large clamps around this assembly with bolts). All this work just for a few nights of thunder.

The old cars were just plain fun. They always had that old car smell of sweat, oil, and exhaust fumes lingering in the upholstery. They were noisy, and they were usually cold in the winter which always brought your lady love closer. The old Blue Streak provided me with many years of pure fun and I still miss that car today. Many years later, I saw an ad in the local paper for a nineteen thirty six two door ford sedan to be auctioned in a week. Sealed bids were being accepted and I couldn't resist, I had to go look at it. When I walked into the room that housed the vehicle, I was astounded, my old Blue Streak was sitting there before me. Only this was a completely restored upgraded Ford. Reupholstered in original cloth, hydraulic brakes, air conditioning. It was a dream come true. I was tempted, but I owned three cars at the time, one of which was a Camaro show car. I didn't have the space to store it and at this point in my life, I knew wouldn't be able to devote the time to the car that it deserved. It was hard to resist, but reason prevailed and I just left when I realized "you cant go home again" I often wondered if it was my old jalopy, but I really didn't want to know. Your first car and your first girl, you just cant forget'em.

Richard T Vogt

7—MY FIRST JOB

November 26, 2013

When I was young, I really didn't have any goal in life. I just wanted to drive my car, hang around with my friends, and hope that once in a while I could experience some excitement and occasionally be lucky enough to have a fling with one of the many sweet girls that were in abundance and seemed only too willing to fulfill my desires. I didn't see myself in the future as the head of some corporation or holding some high political office. I, like most of my friends, knew that when we finished our education, we were expected to find a job and fend for ourselves. That's just the way it was and we accepted it.

Exit high school, get a job. That's where I was at. There were many places to find employment in the area where I lived. In order to make a substantial wage it would be necessary to be willing to do manual labor. There were an abundance of places that required hands on type workers. At the time, the railroad was a major source of employment and there were a couple of automobile manufacturing plants close by. There was a food manufacturing facility in the city that was a huge conglomerate and employed quite a few workers. It was a closed shop in that it was supported by a National Workers Union. Being union, the employees received a high hourly wage and it was just about impossible to get fired. It was a typical labor union utopia waiting for a young guy with little ambition. With benefits like that, it was like having a mermaid lure me onto the rocky shoals and I mustered up the courage to go in for an interview. Much to my surprise, I was hired right on the spot. With much trepidation, I reported to work and my job assignment was in the building that made a gelatin dessert. I had to work under an eager beaver type of guy that I dont think ever smiled or cracked a joke. Strictly business. To top that off, the supervisor was a women that I do believe never met a man she liked.

Of the forty five employees working in the facility, forty two were women. Then there was me, another young guy and the eager beaver.

I was moved around the manufacturing floor and eventually could manage every work assignment with ease. We had an elevator operator in the building with an Irish brogue that knew all the dirty jokes, and when he wasn't telling a joke, he was singing one of the many bawdy ditties that he learned in France during the Big War. To me, it was just a stop over job until I decided what I wanted to do with my life. Most people who worked there were mature company men who intended to stay there and make it a career. The pay was good, the work was steady and that was all most of them were looking for. There were many cases of two generational employment in the ranks and most workers were satisfied. There wasn't any pecking order among the labor force. First man and second man, that was the hierarchy in the labor force. The first man performed the labor and the second man knew why he was doing it. The differential in pay was three dollars and fifty cents an hour more for the second man. He did all the paperwork that accompanied any work assignment.

One day a couple of us crossed swords with our female supervisor over really minor violation of some rule she had established which we considered insignificant. Of course she didn't agree and fired us on the spot. We drove into town and located our union representative at the local Gulf gas station which seemed to be his off site office and pleaded our case by whining and denying we violated any rules. (It helped that the union representative lived in our neighborhood and knew us both since we were toddlers). He quickly contacted the plant manager on the phone and after discussing the incident, told him he wanted us back on the job the next day. When I got home that night, my father told me that someone called from my work place and told him that I was to report to work the next day. When he asked for an explanation, I told him it was just a front office error and and any further discussion of the matter died on the vine.

The following morning I was transferred to one of the five yard gangs whose job was to move various raw materials around the facility. Some of the assignments required loading and unloading empty bottles from freight cars. The bottles were used in the manufacture of either whiskey, gin, or rum. There would be thousands of boxes to transfer. We had a foreman named "Tiny" who happened to have a brother named "Mousie". When the manufacturing schedule slowed down, we would sometimes load the freight cars with cases of bottles we unloaded the night before. Tiny would sometimes release us early and punch everyone out hours later. Sometimes we would work in the whiskey bottling facility where there was a woman who was an empty bottle inspector. The bottles would travel along a conveyor belt and when they got to her work station, they would pass a huge magnifying glass where they would quadriple in size in order to enlarge any defects. With her eyes glued to the speeding bottles, she would reach out when a defect was found, yank the offending bottle off the conveyor belt and smash it in large metal container. I often thought of her when I watched bug eyed Marty Feldman doing his comedy routine.

Workers were always trying to figure out ways to sneak alcoholic beverages through the guarded front gate. Lunch boxes were always searched and any clear liquids were quickly confiscated. They would strap bottles to their body or put home made contraptions under their hat. They had to intercept the booze before it got the government stamp on the cap because after that it would be under federal jurisdiction. But the boys had imagination and were determined in their quest for a free night cap. I knew quite a few of them, and over the years, they had developed a taste for the mind numbing liquid.

The air quality surrounding the manufacturing facility was unpleasant due to a discharge from one of the operations performed when producing yeast cakes which was one of their products. It actually stunk for miles around the area and this occurred almost daily. In those days, it was considered just one of the inconveniences of having a job producer in the area. If something like that happened today, the E.P.A. would on them like a tick on a deer.

They had their own dump on the property which was located on the banks of the river where they would sometimes burn waste products from the various manufacturing operations. At about four in the afternoon, the five yard gangs would always rendezvous there with their trucks to talk over the days events and someone would produce a bottle of contraband gin from their pocket. The boys would all have a snort or two and pass the bottle around. When they passed the bottle to me, I didn't want to appear like a party pooper so I put the bottle to my lips and took generous guzzle. Wow! I could hardly get my breath. The seasoned old timers had a good chuckle at my expense. I don't know how they could drink that stuff but they went at it every day.

I was then assigned to the job of draining the molasses tanks which would take about a week. the molasses was used in the production of one of the alcoholic beverages that was brewed there. I believe it was the rum. The tanks were huge, as big as a house. We would don rubber knee boots and enter the tanks through a circular porthole. We were equipped with a large squeegee attached to a six foot handle. Our assignment was to push the thick molasses toward a drain located on one side of the tank. There were steam lines located about two feet off the floor of the tank which normally maintained a liquid viscosity that would drain the contents by gravity. When the molasses level got below the steam lines, it cooled and wouldn't flow. That's where we came in. The fumes in the tank were so strong that we would get light headed and have to leave and get fresh air. The thick molasses would suck the boots off our feet and we would sometimes step in the sticky goo. Thankfully, the assignment only lasted a week.

Next, I was sent down to the river to unload the grain barges. The tug boat would push the grain barge up to the dock and I would bury the end of a twelve inch vacuum hose deep in the grain. The grain was sucked up through the hose to a storage room with the chaff being blown off on the way up. The chaff dropped down a large tube into a bag which required frequent changing. The wheat was used in the production of whiskey which was also a product of the facility. Caution was needed when putting the vacuum tube into the grain as there was the danger of sinking down into the soft grain.

One day, I felt the patriotic urge to serve my country. The USA had declared a "police action" (war) in North Korea and I knew I had my chance for some excitement. I went down to the recruiting station and joined the US Navy. I served four years in the service of Uncle Sam and when I returned, there was no job waiting for me. The company had reorganized and most of the manufacturing operations were moved elsewhere. But it worked out for the best. I eventually joined the IBM workforce and stayed with them for thirty four years. But my first job is one that I will never forget. I will always have fond memories of Tiny, Mousie, Danny, and the rest of those gin guzzling men of the world.

RichardT Vogt

8—UNCLE SAM WANTS YOU

October 25, 2013

The year was nineteen fifty The big day had arrived, I finally made it. I was graduating from high school. Now it was time for me to go out and make it on my own in that cruel world. No more free meals, free lodging, and free everything. In that time, most graduates didn't give college any consideration. Most of us just went out and got a job at one of the many places that offered employment to unskilled workers. I got a job at a local company that manufactured many different products most of which were in the food line. The pay was good and many of my friends also worked there. But typically, I would get paid on Friday and be broke on Monday. It was a merry go round, every week. I figured I was in a dead end job in a one horse town. Never having traveled any where, I was looking for some excitement out of life, something beyond the everyday grind that afflicted most of the people that I knew. The Korean War had started (I mean the Korean Police Action) and I figured that my uncle Sammy would have an opening for me. I decided to join the United States Navy.

Now this made my father very happy. He was a navy veteran having served on a battleship during the reign of Teddy Roosevelt. Did I say he was happy? I meant ecstatic. Aside from having another son serve in the Navy, he would not have to put up with me coming in at all hours of the night after being involved in behavior he really didn't approve of. He gave me his blessing and I was on my way. I went down to the recruiting station with a friend of mine and we both signed up for a four year hitch. (Or so I thought) I ran into this same friend of mine about a year after I enlisted and he was wearing an army uniform. Who knew?

In those times, the recruiter painted a rosy picture for new recruits." You want electronics school? Sure, and you'll get it". "Want duty on an aircraft carrier? No problem, your uncle will take care of you." I first had to tie up any loose ends at home before leaving such as giving my brother in law my cherished first car with the agreement that I would have full use of it when I got home on leave. I had to bid my true love goodby and promise her that I would stay true. She did the same for me but I quickly found out that devotion wasn't one of her strong points. This was a big step for me. I had never been more than ten miles from home in my life. I hoped I could control the trepidation that I felt oozing from my pores.

The big day arrived and my father, looking as proud as a peacock, accompanied me down to New York City where I would be inducted. I was met at Grand Central Station by a swabbie who would escort me and quite a few potential sailor boys over to 39 Whitehall Street where we would get our indoctrination. To say I was nervous would be like saying a condemned man standing on the gallows with a noose around his neck was concerned. We were separated into small groups and escorted to waiting buses that took us over to Whitehall Street. The location was a military induction center that had been in use for that purpose since the eighteen hundreds. Up to this point, all the naval personnel assigned to us were polite and reassuring. As I looked over the assembly of potential gobs, I saw many different types that were being inducted. They were from all over New York State. The upstate farm-boys were easily spotted by their clothing. there were bookish types and of course the big city boys all strutting their stuff, cracking jokes and jockeying for position of "leader of the pack" But it was evident to anyone with any insight that the veneer of cockiness they had erected around themselves was just exposing their insecurity. We were all scared!

Once we arrived at the induction center we were given a battery of physical and physiological tests to determine if we were suitable for cannon fodder. I don't know who coined the phrase "All men are created equal" But I'm sure that person never took a physical for military service.

Part of the physiological test was to inquire whether or not we liked girls. I didn't see anyone rejected at that point in the testing so I figured I was with a bunch of casanova's. We were still being treated with kid gloves by the sailors herding us from one station to the next and I started to get suspicious. Eyes, ears, noses. They were probing all the orifices of our bodies trying to find something that would eliminate us from the pack assembled there. We were there for most of the day, standing around in groups most of the time. I got to know a few of the guys in the group and I found that they were just like me, looking for a little excitement and trying to expand their horizons. The ones that I talked to all made it a point to show me pictures of their girlfriends while some told me of their future plans with their sweetie. You know, little cottage with a picket fence, kids on a swing in the back yard, mommy with the apron waiting for him to come home from work. In most cases, that vision would materialize but without him in the picture. I saw dear John letters break a lot of hearts during my enlistment.

We finally got to the point where we were about to be sworn in. That meant we would become the property of the U.S. Government. We were informed that anyone not wishing to become a sailor should leave the room before the swearing in ceremony. Then we were all told to stand at attention and raise our right hand. As we were sworn in, I could feel a change come over me. I felt my freedom disappear. I couldn't quit this job. This was for keeps. It was too late to decide if I had made a mistake. I noticed a change in the demeanor of the sailors herding us around now. They were more authoritative, more demanding, telling us not asking us. Your'e in the navy now son! I thought it ironic that now I would once again be getting free food, free lodging, free everything. Vot a country! They put us on a train at Grand Central Station for the ride up to New England where we would finish the journey to our new home on a bus.

We arrived in Providence about midnight and just sat around waiting for a bus to the training base in Newport Rhode Island. It was obvious that the Navy didn't have much pull with the bus company. I thought that government buses would be used to transport us, but it didn't work out that way. We arrived at the base about four in the morning and were told to get off the bus and stand at attention. They gave us each a blanket, mattress cover and pillow and took us to the barracks building that would be home for the next three months. We all figured that they would let us sleep late, but we got our first taste of navy life at five thirty in the morning with a shrill whistling noise that we found out was the way they woke you in the navy. A boson's pipe. That was the way our every move was directed, a boson's pipe. We were assigned to a chief petty officer named Barclay. He was a real old salt with twenty six years in the navy. He would be our lord and master for the next three months.

He got us on deck and assembled outside and marched us down to the chow hall. I will never forget the aromas of different foods wafting in the air as we arrived at the hall. It was the most cavernous eating hall I had ever seen. I noticed the seasoned recruits eating at the mess hall eying us with an air of disdain. Marching back to the barracks, this same bunch hurled a few cutting remarks at us as we passed them. When we arrived at the barracks our navy life began. The first thing they did was cut our hair, right down to the skin. An interview and then we got our necessities such as clothes and sea bag. The chief then picked out a few of the bigger guys and promoted them to "recruit petty officer", really a title with little authority. They were responsible to do the leg work for the chief and used as whipping boys when we didn't hit the mark. The first night we slept in the barracks, I heard a few of the homesick boys sobbing in their bunks. I figured that at times like this it was good to be a motherless child.

It was difficult getting used to living with one hundred twenty other guys, but boot training was good. I was accepted into the recruit training drum and bugle corps as a drummer and was excused from Saturday morning inspections. When we were given training in marching, it didn't usually last long. The chief would have us stack our rifles and he would regale us with sea stories from the second world war. He was an interesting guy with a lot of tales. At the rifle range, we were given minimal instruction. I guess the marines were the hot shots in that area. The chief was instructing us in the manual of arms one day and a recruit in the ranks was goofing off. The chief called him up front and told him that if he knew so much about rifle drill he could instruct the class. He went through some fancy maneuvers with that piece like I had never seen before. He finished the class for the chief.

Most of our classroom instructions were movies. In many classes the instructor would flip the overhead lights on halfway through the movie and catch half of us asleep. We would then have to stand at attention at the back of the room for the remainder of the movie. They even had a movie on the proper techniques to use when making out with a girl. Most of the instructors were swabbies just finishing up their hitch waiting to get discharged so their heart really wasn't in the game anymore. Three months without seeing a girl. Now that was cruel and unusual punishment. I guess they were just trying to get us to adjust to separation anxiety when we went out to sea.

All recruits had to do a tour of mess cooking. That is working in or around the kitchen. I was doing my tour serving the food to the recruits in the mess hall and one day they had strawberries. Three of us each took a bowl and hid it away so we could have them after they stopped serving food. This had to be the one day that they ran out of desert which meant some recruits didn't get their strawberries. When we were cleaning up, the master at arms (usually a third class petty officer with about forty years in the navy) discovered our bowls of strawberries hidden under the counter. Well, it was the Caine Mutiny all over again. (Do you remember Bogart?) We scrubbed garbage cans all week as punishment.

Well, I broke boots as they say and now I was a full fledged sailor The first thing I did was to get a tattoo. I was now going to a duty station where I would serve my four year enlistment, but that is another story for another time.

Richard (Digger) Vogt

9—A SWIM IN BARCELONA BAY

6-20-2013

Join the navy and see the world!! So proclaimed the ad at the post office. I did and I did. I was a sailor in the US Navy during the Korean war. I served on a destroyer which is a small, fast, anti submarine vessel with a crew of about three hundred. The ship was always on the go and I had a lot of sea time which enabled me to travel to far away places and see a lot of the world. During this period of my life, I experienced a lot of incidents which when looked back on now, have a humorous side to them. One such incident started out as just a few swabbies out on the town in Barcelona Spain.

After a few weeks out to sea and no contact with anyone except crew mates, liberty in any port means a chance to try out those sea legs on land and get acquainted with the local wild life, which in this case is members of the opposite sex. The four of us invaded the city of Barcelona intent on spending our time and money on wine, women, and song. We always figured we would tour the cultural points of Spain when we came back as tourists sometime in the future. Needless to say, no one has more fun than sailors on liberty in a new port of call.

After we had visited most of the establishments of entertainment and renewed our faith in the ability of a woman to rejuvenate a lonely sailor, we headed back to our ship full of confidence and Barcelona bubbly. Upon arriving back at the dock where our ship was tied up, I longed for some more of the fun we were having a short time ago. Well, my shipmates who were with me had a different plan and that was to get aboard ship. As we were going up the gangway to the ship, I bolted for the taxi on the dock and my buddies grabbed my arm and tried to pull me aboard the ship. In all this confusion, the railing on the gangway separated and I went down, down, down into the dark, icy waters of Barcelona bay. As I dropped down between the pilings and the ship I could hear my shipmates calling words of encouragement which really didn't do much to bolster my confidence.

The officer of the deck (O. D.) was an ensign fresh out of school who was responsible for extracting me from my predicament. The spotlights went on and a rope ladder was tossed over the side to enable me to climb aboard. Climb a rope ladder? Never happen!!. I still wonder how I was able to stay afloat. It just happened that another shipmate was arriving from liberty and he didn't give it much thought, he just dove in with me. Now there are two of us foundering around in murky water and an ensign who had never studied situations like this in officers school. Well, they tossed down a length of rope and the swab in the water with me tied it around my middle and I was hauled back aboard still wearing my flat hat.

After I had cleaned up, I went to sleep in the machine shop and was awakened by the J.O.D. and told to report to the ships chief corpsman (pseudo doctor). He asked how I felt and I told him I had a sore on my lip, and that was a mistake. He ripped into me about how he was just curious about my condition after the swimming incident and not interested in my (bleep) love life. I guess he was really sore about being awakened at four am for what he considered an irresponsible swabbies mishap.

I learned that the O.D. had put me on report which meant I would have to go to executive officers mast which is a navy shipboard court. Now there are a lot of seasoned, salty sailors aboard any ship and they were quick to advise me how to "beat the rap". Most of them were "lifers" and had been through the wringer many times themselves. I listened to the many scenarios they wove to prove I was just a victim and decided that I would have an easy time before the exec. I was sure I was going to pull the rabbit out my hat!!

A few weeks later it was show time! I went before the exec on the quarterdeck where he sat in the doorway of the post office to hold court. After my division officer spoke of my good record (I received the good conduct medal the prior week) and my exemplary work ethic, I stated my case which unfortunately at the time sounded very weak. Well, that executive officer climbed up one side of me and down the other like a Himalayan Sherpa and I knew right then and there that I wouldn't step foot on land for awhile (thirty days aboard ship to be exact). But then again, even those thirty days were a lot of fun. Its hard to extinguish the zest for fun in a young sailor!! I went on to more adventures aboard that ship and ended up with a treasure trove of memories that are with me to this day. (60 years later)

Richard T Vogt

10—SHORE PATROL

Dcember 7, 2013

I served in the U.S. Navy during the Korean war and I would like to relate to you my experiences while serving shore patrol duty both domestically and in some of the foreign ports I visited.

The armed forces of the United States have their own police forces. The Army has military police who are specially trained to carry out the duties of law enforcement and are permanently assigned to this task. The Air Force has specially trained personnel who are also permanently assigned to law enforcement. These men go to school to learn how to perform the duties necessary to be air policemen. The Navy, however uses both permanent and part time personnel to patrol the streets whenever Navy men are at liberty on shore. The full time shore patrol (Navy police) are provided special schooling to be able to maintain order on the streets of any port of call and to effect an arrest and apprehension in cases where they deem it necessary. The part time Navy shore patrol is chosen from the ranks of petty officers on a rotating schedule. They are not sent to school nor do they get any special training on how to perform their duties while serving as policemen for the Navy. They are however always teamed up with permanent shore patrol who always take the initiative in cases where action is required.

I was in the Navy about a year and a half before I was promoted to the rank of petty officer. This promotion obligated me to serve shore patrol duty at random. When I reported for my first assignment, I was in a group of hapless sailors who were not really looking forward to being Navy policeman. We were all provided with the equipment needed to carry out our duties as shore patrolmen which included an arm band emblazoned with large S P letters in bold red, a wooden club, and a white garrison belt. We were told to use the club only for protection and never hit anyone above the neck. The elbows, knees and wrists were the vital points to strike if necessary. The Chief Petty Officer in charge of the duty section looked us over, briefed us on military protocol for Navy shore patrol, and after assigning each of us to a permanent shore patrol sailor, handed out the assignments for the section of town that we would be patrolling for the night. When I got my assignment, I noticed a look of relief come over the rest of the group. I found out that I had pulled duty in the black section of town which was considered to be hazardous. That's right, in the fifties, even staid old Newport practiced segregation for the Saturday night Navy social gatherings.

Before we departed for our duty sections, the chief in charge showed us a photo of a sailor and told us he was wanted for being A.W.O.L. which in civilian lingo means absent without official leave. It was a serious offense. He also told us the man was armed and dangerous and would require more than one man to bring him in if he was spotted. As soon as I got on the street, a change came over me., Decked out in my shore patrol accessories, I was no longer a skinny kid who avoided confrontation, but a big man with power over other people. I often wondered if everyone was affected that way. About midnight, my partner told me to check the locker rooms at the Y.M.C.A. When I entered the first room, I spotted a sailor unconscious laying face down on the floor. I was certain it was the desperado the chief told us to look for. I reported to my partner who enlisted two more shore patrolmen and we went to get him. When he was prodded with a foot to the body, he came up cursing, swinging and wielding a knife. I swung my club and got him in the wrist which released his grip on the weapon he was carrying. We put him in the patrol wagon and he was carted off to the brig. (jail) I never did find out if he was the wanted man. I also had duty in Newport another night where I was assigned to "early riot squad". Riot squads are a group of shore patrolmen that sit around and wait for a fight to erupt in one of the many bars in any Navy town. The Navy has the squads not only to break up fights in bars but to protect the sailors from local policemen who usually just don't appreciate the enrichment that the swabbies bring to their town. In Norfolk, there used to be signs "Sailors and Dogs, Keep off the

Grass" Norfolk was known to the sailors as s—t city. There is an early riot squad group and a late riot squad group. Early riot squad duty is much better. Fewer riots. When sailors from the south get drinking together with sailors from the north, it's usually a Civil War battle all over again. But this time the shore patrol always wins!

I was assigned shore patrol duty again in Singapore which is located in Southeast Asia off the coast of Malaysia. When I was there, poverty was rampant and the natives eyed foreigners with suspicion. When standing shore patrol in a foreign country, it was customary to team up with the local police or military while patrolling. Luckily, the policeman I patrolled with spoke a little English so we didn't have a communication problem. We both intended not only to protect the natives from drunken unruly sailors, but to protect those same sailors from the natives who fell into the category of the have-nots. But, its impossible to be everywhere so when three sailors came up to us and told us that their cameras had been stolen, it didn't surprise me. The policeman I was patrolling with was furious and it was obvious that crime against visitors was not tolerated by the authorities in Singapore. We went to the local police station where a report was filed and then after supplementing our group with two detectives, we went into what I considered a ghetto area. The detectives seemed to know the thieves based on the description supplied by the sailors. We went directly to a run down shack that was occupied by a family and the detectives aggressively questioned the occupants. Then they proceeded to tear the place apart and finally, hidden behind a pile of rubble were the cameras. They roughly shoved two of the occupants of the shack, who were men, into the police van and transported them to the jail. Meanwhile, an officer from our ship arrived on the scene and was told that the men would be tried in court the next day and the sailors who were robbed would have to testify. The officer got approval from the captain and agreed to delay the ship's departure for a day. The men were tried and convicted the next day. Justice was swift in Singapore. I felt sorry for the men, they were just wretched individuals with no hope for a future. Caning was a form of punishment in Singapore in those days and I wondered if that was the sentence they received. Our ship got underway the next day for a new adventure.

When we anchored in Kure Japan, I was assigned to shore patrol again and walked the beat with an Australian sailor who was much older than me and was a career navy man. I noticed that the Aussies didn't hesitate to use their clubs when one of their men got rowdy. Whenever they encountered an uncooperative Australian swabbie, they would simply knock them over the head with the club and toss them into the jeep for transport to the brig. I took a more temperate approach to maintaining the peace. While I was in Kure, I traveled down to see the ruins of Hiroshima.

The city was leveled, nothing standing. I couldn't imagine anything like it. The Japanese people living near the location purposely avoided eye contact with us and it was easy to see the fear and resentment that they harbored for their conquerors. Our stay in Kure was quiet, a shore patrol dream.

We stopped at Manila and Subic Bay in the Philippines and I pulled shore patrol in the latter city. It was an underdeveloped place with dirt roads and bars that were makeshift structures intended to relieve the sailors of their money. Whenever we arrived at a port where there wasnt much entertainment, we knew that shore patrol duty would be difficult. Alcohol and prostitutes are two of the ingredients needed to make trouble. While patrolling the streets, a local madam came out of one of the bawdy houses frantically waving her arms and screaming. It seemed that a sailor was not satisfied with the merchandise he purchased and refused to pay for it. When we entered the establishment there was a partially clad rather large sailor tearing the place up while the girls ran screaming for cover. We attempted to reason with him, but he was adamant in his refusal to pay for faulty merchandise. We finally maneuvered him into a corner of the room and all charged him at once. It was no contest, he caved when we all piled on. He reluctantly agreed to compensate the madam and apologize to the girl if we didn't charge him but we still had a problem. His pants had somehow disappeared. We managed to find a pair of civilian pants to cover him up and finally put him in the jeep for the trip back to his ship. I'm sure the officer of the deck on his ship added this to his "never in my life" book.

Richard T Vogt

11—CROSSING THE EQUATOR

November 20, 2013

I served four years in the U S Navy and and was stationed on the destroyer USS Brownson, a small ship with a crew of about three hundred men. It was a well armed ship and was built as a hunter killer vessel. That is to say we searched for and sunk submarines. It was equipped with torpedoes, depth charges, anti aircraft guns and guns for purposes of shore bombardment. We were anchored out in the Narragansett bay getting the ship prepared for a cruise that would include a tour of duty off the coast of North Korea and eventually take us around the world.

We had one young kid aboard the ship who was recently married and really didn't want to go on the mission. One day, while he was painting the bow of the ship, he just jumped off the scaffolding screaming and started swimming out into the bay. They sent the whaleboat out to retrieve him and we never saw that sailor again. Most of us were looking forward to the day we weighed anchor. I was mess cooking at that time. That meant I was working with the galley crew preparing and serving the meals. This was an assignment that everyone that wasn't a rated petty officer had to rotate through for a limited amount of time. I was designated the "salad king" which meant I had to prepare three trays of salad for the dinner serving. Some worked the steam tables, in the scullery, or assisted the cooks in the galley. The job I had was one of the best. On a ship, they have a "water king" who has the responsibility of maintaining the water tank levels, and an "oil king" who is responsible for keeping the fuel tanks full. I would get real creative with the salads, garnishing them with pimentos and anchovies much to the delight of the ravenous crew members. It was the best job I had all during during my four year hitch.

But it didn't last long enough. I was promoted to Third Class Petty Officer which meant I had to relinquish my crown to a lesser man. My specialty was diesel engines which didn't require much effort on my part being that the ship was propelled by steam power. I stood watches in the engine room where we would bake potatoes on the steam lines and make a delicious pot of potato soup on the night watch. We would go to the galley at night when the baker was baking bread and try to mooch some fresh bread to go with our soup. If the baker refused, we would cut off the fresh air vents to the galley and he would soon come around to our way of thinking. The heat below decks was stifling which meant the regulations for uniforms were less strict than those above deck. When we would take on stores from a supply depot or supply ship, all hands would be required to turn to (work) loading the food onto the ship. The black gang (below deck personnel, who are also referred to as snipes by the rest of the crew) always managed to drop a few canned hams and cases of tuna fish down the hatches to the snipes waiting below. Sometimes the supply officer would notice the missing items and search the engine rooms, but there were too many hiding places in the bilges and he never recovered anything. When he and his men entered the engine room, they were as out of place as cowboys at a ballet recital.

We would cross the equator on this voyage and it would entail an elaborate ceremony. The rites date back to the days of wooden ships and iron men. It requires a lot of preparation If a man has not been across the equator, he is a "pollywog" and when the crossing day arrives, he is in for a brutal initiation. This applies to all crew members. If the captain of the ship hasn't been across, he to is subject to the punishment meted out. It starts about two weeks before the crossing date when all the leftover food from the mess line is stored in garbage cans.

This includes food scraped from the crew members mess trays. On the day of the crossing, a sort of tunnel is constructed by the shellbacks (those who have crossed before) out of a canvas tarpaulin on the weather deck of the ship and all this rotten, smelly, food waste is thrown in the tunnel. The unbearable heat at the equator only makes the shellbacks happier and the contents of the tunnel more rancid. The night before the crossing, King Neptune contacts the ship and notifies the captain that he will be boarding the ship the following morning to initiate the rotten, slimy, no good pollywogs.

When the day of the crossing arrives, King Neptune and Davy Jones emerge from the deep to take command of the ship. (These roles are played by shellbacks). All of the pollywogs are awakened to an abusive diatribe over the loudspeakers and are stuffed into the mess deck area. They are given saltine crackers and water for breakfast and told to wait until their name is called. All of the fresh air blowers are shut off and they sit there and swelter in the tropical heat.

Some of those waiting are terror stricken, having been told by the shellbacks of the horrors that await them during the ceremony to follow, and are nervous as a cat in a chinese restaurant.

Meanwhile there is an assembly of shellbacks on the fantail (back) of the ship dressed in costumes representing various characters involved in the crossing, and they do mean business! Those shellbacks not playing roles are dressed in bizarre outfits. Torn shirts, a patch over an eye like a pirate, a big gold earring, Sabres hanging from their waists, the uniform code was rescinded for the duration of the crossing ceremony.

As each man's name is called, he emerges from the mess hall and starts crawling on his hands and knees over abrasive deck treads through a gauntlet of shellbacks wielding foot long pieces of wet canvas fire hose which they will use to vigorously apply punishment to the pollywogs buttocks. The first trial is the "tunnel of love" which contains the spoiled smelly garbage They must crawl through on their hands and knees. Many upchuck when emerging from the tunnel where they are greeted by a blast from a fire hose. And then they have to crawl some more to kiss the belly of the royal baby. This role is played by the fattest shellback with the largest belly which is smeared with mustard. Their face is usually pushed into the mustard by an overzealous shellback who remembers the punishment he took when he was a pollywog. Then they have to crawl some more, usually on bleeding knees, to kiss the foot of the sea hag. They are then confronted by the royal doctor and given a small cup of liquid which they are told to drink. At this point, the mental state of many of the inductees is sheer panic. Next, it is on to kiss King Neptune's ring. A large vat of sea water has been placed on deck where the pollywog is seated in a chair. The royal barber cuts a swath of hair off right down the middle of his head just before he is dumped backwards into the vat of water where he is held under. When he does come up for air, he is asked by the dunkers, "pollywog or shellback"? Answer "shellback" and you're free to go. Mumble" pollywog" and it's back under water.

When I completed the ceremony, I felt seasick and couldn't figure it out. Remember the magic potion the royal doctor gave us to drink? It was an antidote for ingesting poison which induced vomiting. I raced to the head (bathroom) and was greeted by the sounds of mass dry heaves. Remember what we had for breakfast? I was now officially a "shellback" and initiated into "The Ancient Order Of The Deep" and received a certificate to prove it. We also crossed the international date line and got inducted into the" Domain Of The Golden Dragon" for which we received another certificate. The third honor which we received was to be inducted into the "Ancient Order Of Magellan" to commemorate going around the world, and of course, another certificate. Most of us weren't dry behind the ears yet, but we really felt like old salts and had the swagger to prove it when we went on shore liberty. I have known sailors who served twenty years aboard ships and never got a chance to achieve any of these goals.

While serving our tour in North Korea, We would periodically go to Japan for R&R. This is what the navy called "rest and recuperation" we used to refer to it as "rape and rampage" We would stay there for a week and then go go back to our tour of duty. It was shortly after the end of WW2 and I felt that the Japanese people were in awe of the big bad Americans and really treated us as liberators rather than conquerors. After leaving Korea, we encountered a typhoon in the China Sea that tossed our little ship around like a cork. I never saw such huge waves. We rode that storm out for three days and were lucky not to have suffered severe damage to the ship. At night we would strap ourselves into our bunks so we wouldn't get thrown out and injured.

We anchored out in the harbor in Hong Kong China where Mary Soo and her sidecleaners were hired to clean the sides of the ship. This was a navy tradition when in the port. Mary Soo had about twenty young girls working for her. The only compensation she received for all their labor was the right to sell Coca Cola to the crew and to salvage all the waste food from our meals. We just scraped the food from our trays into a large can and they dined on it. Now that is adversity! The Orient seemed to have the power to make sailors gravitate to tattoo parlors. I went ashore with two guys who were yet to be marked for life. One of them got a cross eyed duck on one shoulder and another on the other shoulder calling out "Hey You! Who Me?" I wonder if my buddy thinks of me when he looks at those Daffy Ducks? A large cobra adorns the arm of the other swab. I had received a dear John letter from my true love while in Korea so I figured "I'll show her" and had her name tattoo'd on my arm. (In Japanese). We were all in for a shock when we awoke the next morning.

Once we were homeward bound, we made stops in various countries to act as good will ambassadors for America. We tied up in Singapore where we were greeted by Chinese tailors from Hong Kong China who would measure us up for new civilian clothing at ridiculous prices. When we got to Hong Kong a week later, our new zoot suits and jackets were ready. In France we bought gallons of Chanel No. Five which was probably just colored water. An officer aboard ship purchased a Vespa motor scooter in Italy and brought it home on the ship. Japanese kimonos for the ladies were hanging all over the compartments on the ship. We were a seagoing gift shop. We spent a lot of money and had a lot of fun. I don't know if the boys from the "Bouncin' Brownson" helped diplomatic relations abroad, but we certainly tried!

Richard T Vogt

12—JIMMY'S BRASS RAIL

November 14, 2013

Jimmy's Brass Rail was a bar / restaurant that was owned by a good friend of mine where everyone always knew everyone else that patronized the place. It was sort of a home away from home. A place where you could go and always feel welcome and get into a friendly conversation on almost any subject. If solitude was what you were after, you could always find it there. Jimmy purchased the place from a real estate icon who was a big player in the town in which it was located. I was told by a reliable source that he got a deal on the place that a person wouldn't normally offer to his own mother. Now, that's a good deal! Jimmy's family had been in the bar / restaurant business for years and I think this was a factor that influenced the sale to him. Jimmy knew that this change in his life could put him on easy street for a long time.

It was a good sized place with about fifteen booths for dining and a well equipped kitchen that was supervised by his mother and his wife. They were both excellent cooks and the place did a thriving business. There was a shuffleboard table located in the bar area which was well used and sold a lot of drinks which the loser in the match usually bought. Darts were a popular game and drew in a lot of the better dart players in town. A lot of money was made and lost at the dart board. Out of town sharpies would come to Jimmy's just to show up the local masters of the feathered projectiles.

What really gave the bar its allure was the collection of customers that were usually there every day seeking companionship and a refuge from the everyday repetition of their boring lives which drive most people to desperation. There was one fellow who worked as a gandy dancer on the railroad. A gandy dancer was a slang term term for a person who walked the rails every day looking for loose spikes which held the rail to the tie. Any that he found were quickly driven back into the railroad tie with a sledgehammer that he carried over his shoulder. I was in my twenties then and he looked like an old man to me. He followed the same routine every day. He would stop in for one beer on the way home, go home and clean up before he ate and then return to chug beer all night. He was about the best shuffleboard player in the place. The bar sponsored a team which used to travel to a town across the Hudson River to play in tournaments. I remember a bunch of us going across the river on the ferry boat and singing with the accompaniment of an accordion played by one of the team. We had great times.

There was Danny, who used to pass out on the bar just about every night. I don't know where this guy worked, but he must have had a prince for a boss. Another guy used to go in the kitchen at night and make himself a Bermuda onion sandwich on rye bread. Needless to say, he was never a big hit with the ladies that frequented the place. And there was a little guy that drove a cab. Every morning at about eight o'clock he would double park his cab and come in for a shot of whiskey and a beer chaser. He used to say that it cleared the cobwebs from his brain. He chased those cobwebs all day long. There was a bookie who use to come in at about noon to pick up some action from the high rollers betting on the horses running in the Big Apple. (more about that later) It was the kind of place where you could always find a couple of guys willing to help you move your refrigerator or even find a crowd ready to do some heavy lifting if you were moving. If you needed a few bucks to hold you over till payday, usually someone would come up with the green. No class distinction. Somehow, alcohol has always been the common denominator. Bottom rung or top of the ladder, so what? Everyone got along and it was always party time. There was no need for Annie's List, if you needed some work done by a craftsman, there was always someone with a recommendation. In fact, some of Jimmy's customers were skilled in their trade. A quick meal that was always advertised in the bar was a "boneless chicken dinner for five cents" Usually it was ordered by someone who was not a regular at the bar. When they ordered it they were given a small plate holding a hard boiled egg, a napkin, and a knife and fork. Oh, they were also given a saltshaker. This always got a laugh out of everyone there.

One day, the bartender got in a discussion with a patron about the spelling of the word prerogative. The patron insisted it was spelled P.E.R.O.G.A.T.I.V.E. Everyone in the place got in the act and gave their expert opinions. This went on for about an hour and finally the bartender sent someone to the store for a dictionary. There was a wager on the outcome, drinks on the house. Much to the dismay of the patron, he lost and the beer drinkers all switched to top shelf scotch.

One of the bartenders was a teetotaler, having given up the demon rum years earlier, though he never looked down on those with a yen for the spirits. He would usually send someone out for ice cream sodas every night much to the amusement of the beer guzzlers in the house. But one night he got into the booze and went on a rampage that just about wrecked the bar. The incident took everyone by surprise. Needless to say, he was relieved of his duties and went into another line of work. The second bartender employed there was named Moony and he was straight from county cork in Ireland. He parted his hair in the middle and wore his white apron up high almost to his chest so that he resembled a server from the gay ninety's era. He was very quiet and stingy with his conversation but was a good listener which is essential in the business of bar tending. One day he found it necessary to eject a young lady from the premises for unruly behavior and when she got to the door he told her not to return. With that, she placed her hand on the door knob, turned around hurled a flurry of profanity at him that would make a truck driver blush. Unabashed, Moony just went about his duties as the customers at the bar roared with laughter.

One of the regulars got the idea one day to start a cork club. Anyone joining the club would be given a plain cork from a wine bottle and they would need to have it on their person whenever they entered the bar. If they were asked to show their cork and couldn't produce it, it cost them a dime. That person would have to toss a dime overhead to a fake ceiling above the bar that was built of glass. The fake ceiling had back lighting so that the coins were visible in silhouette when seated at the bar. A clambake was planned for the club members in the closed bar whenever a sufficient amount of money was collected to cover the cost. All the regulars were in on it. It resulted in a lot of fun over the next few months and the accumulation of coins was considerable. When it got to a point where no light was coming through the overhead glass they figured it was time for a good old fashioned clambake.

A few guys got up there, scraped the coins together and much to their surprise they found that they had enough to finance a clambake. One hundred fifty dollars. (remember, beer was fifteen cents a glass) so that was a lot of money in those days. Now the planning began and the planning went on, and on, and on. Finally Jimmy reluctantly admitted that he had squandered the money and that there would be no clambake. Some took it in stride, others left never to return to the place they knew so well.

Jimmy got a gold mine when he bought that bar. All he had to do was keep working the mother lode, but he ran into two obstacles to his success. Horses and women! I don't think he ever met a women that he didn't like or a horse that wasn't a sure thing. He used to con the bookmaker on the daily doubles by having a plant at a diner outside the track who would call the first horse in the double to someone at his bar and they would play the double with the bookie who usually came in after the first race was run. They cut their odds of losing in half this way. But like most people who play the ponies, he ended up with a pocket full of betting stubs. He just couldn't resist the lure of curvaceous body on a woman or those juicy red lips beckoning him. As a result, he didn't pay attention to his business. And then it happened! Two men came into the place one day and announced that they were tax agents from the state and were going to padlock the place because of non payment of state taxes. It was a devastating blow not only to Jimmy, but to all of the people who patronized the place and found refuge there. The good times were over! Jimmy never entered into any other type of business venture and the bar never reopened. I guess the moral of the story here is "never play the ponies to make a profit and keep your horse in the barn.

Richard T Vogt

13—BLUE TIME

December 28, 2013

When I was discharged from the U S Navy after the Koran War, I didn't go back to my original place of employment, a local manufacturing facility where I was employed right out of high school. On the advice of a friend, I decided to seek employment at a facility that made computers which was located upstate from where lived. When I went there to submit an application, I found that the plant had very tight security because of the government contracts they were involved with. It was completely surrounded by a high chain link fence and the entrances were guarded. When I drove up to the guard shack to find out where I would go to submit an application, the guard told me to drive around to the back where the personnel department was located. I got in my car, drove through the gate to the back where I encountered a dead end of chain link fence. I drove back to the front, got out of my car, walked over to the guard shack and asked how I could get to the personnel department. When the guard saw my car inside the fence, he came rushing out of the shack with arms flying, veins bulging on his neck and his eyes bulging out so far that you could hang your hat on them. "How did you get in there, he demanded". "Get that car out of there before I lose my job". Obviously, security was sorely lacking at the facility!

I went in, applied, and subsequently was called back for a series of interviews. At one of interviews, I stated that I had doubts about working for a company so large, that I might get lost in the shuffle. The interviewer looked me straight in the eye and said, "son, there are no lost souls working for this company". He was so sincere, he sold me right on the spot. That was really my first full time job and the only job I would have for the rest of my life. I was employed there for thirty four years.

It was a manufacturing facility and had an assembly line where they conducted "time studies". Wasted motion was eliminated. People that did the studies were called efficiency experts,. and efficient they were. If an operator moved his hand to place a screw on a frame, they would have him perform an operation with the same hand on the return swing. no wasted motion.

I started working on the machine floor for forty two dollars a week. I was repetitious work that usually required standing for eight hours. We put the finishing touches on manufactured parts before they were installed in the finished product. Although it wasn't piece work, a certain number of parts were expected to be produced every hour. I was working on a machine one night and ran a drill through my hand. I went to the dispensary where the nurse on duty was more nervous than I was and sent me to a local hospital where they stitched me up and sent me back to the plant. When my manager asked if I wanted to go home, I declined and stayed to finish up my shift. Now that is the gung-ho attitude of a new employee. If that happened in the work climate of today, there would be a workman's compensation claim followed by a long hiatus from work by the employee to allow him time to retain a lawyer for the lawsuit which would surely follow. I enjoyed working on the machine floor and the people that I worked with although it was hot, oily work. But a new technology was emerging and I wanted to be a part of it. Semiconductors were becoming a big part of the business and I made a move to the white lab coat environment where instead of using tools, we used tweezers. No more punch presses or grinding wheels, it was bell jars and zone levelers that required very little labor but a lot of vigilance. There was a lot of microscope work which was hard on the eyes and again the repetition of the work made it difficult to tolerate. An opening came about in one of the outlying laboratory buildings where they were setting up a complete new experimental development line for masking devices and I managed to land a position on that project. The process was in it's infancy and offered an opportunity for innovation. As we developed the process I discovered new ways to fabricate the product that we needed and in doing so, the company responded with many awards. The company was very liberal in rewarding employees for a job well done. Again, I was satisfied on my job, but in order to fatten up the pay check, it was necessary to join the boys with the wing tipped shoes. The engineering force. At that time, dark suits, white shirts, and dark ties were the uniform of the day, and don't let your hair grow too long. A desk job meant you were a thinker and that was the motto of the company. The people on the manufacturing line knew how to do a job, but the desk jockeys knew why they were doing it. That meant the difference in pay scales.

The company was fair, but paternalistic in it's policies. Cheating on your wife? Your manager will take you to the woodshed if he finds out. Stopping at your favorite watering hole to tip back a few on payday? Don't even think of cashing your check there! But when you landed a job with the company, you were considered to be set for life. If you had a job sweeping the floors, your parents would go around boasting of your good fortune to be working there. I stayed with the company for thirty four years and I still think it was a great place to work.

It got to a point where automation was rapidly replacing people and the company had to reduce the size of the workforce. They were coming out with early retirement incentives that were getting hard to refuse. Finally, they came out with a plan that I just couldn't turn down.

I talked it over with my wife who would still be employed while I would be idle and she agreed that it was the right thing to do. On the day I retired, I told my manager to have the paperwork done by eleven fifty five in the morning as I had a limousine picking me up at the main entrance. He scoffed at me, but at noon, he walked me to the main entrance and there was a limo with my wife waiting for me. That was one of greatest days of my life. Its funny, I drove down past the plant about a week later, and it was as if I never worked there. How soon we forget!

Richard T Vogt

14—ROE HOOK ADVENTURE

Many years ago in another time, it was pretty common for young men to go out on a date and then park their cars to spoon with their girlfriends. This was done with no fear of assailants in the night creating havoc. However there was another danger that was ever present and could turn a night of amore into a nightmare. The danger was—A WEAK CAR BATTERY!!!!! Let me tell you of an instance that caused a nightmare for me and my friend and also a few people who were completely oblivious of the situation.

It was a nice balmy summer night and myself and my date had just completed an evening of dining and dancing. It seemed to me to be a great idea to go park in one of the local "lovers lanes" with this sweet lady and talk about the future. Now, lovers lanes in those days were abundant and completely safe from marauders. The place I chose was known as Roe Hook. It was a narrow dirt road that led to an abandoned Railway station on the Hudson river that was once used to move troops to and from a nearby military base. Along this dirt road were areas where roadway brush had been trampled down which allowed a car to back in the space. There were probably a dozen spaces and they were usually filled nightly with romantic romeos and their ladies fair. The aroma of fragrant wild blossoms mixed with soft music on the radio and a favorite girl in your arms. What more could a young lothario ask for, the world was his oyster.

Well, about midnight, I figured I was about two hours over this young ladies curfew and that I should get her home in a hurry. Unfortunately, my car battery didn't agree with me. The soft music playing for hours on the radio had drained its power and the car wouldn't start, uh oh!!!!!! The parking spots were all deserted and it was really dark. We started walking down the dirt road to the paved highway about a half mile away. We managed to flag down a good Samaritan with a sense of humor and rode to the town where I placed my by now terrified friend in a cab and sent her on her way home. (glad I didn't have to face the wrath of her parents.) Now I had to figure a way to retrieve the car with the dead battery (which belonged to my brother in law who was working late and expected me to pick him up at his restaurant)

I had a brother who drove a bakery truck on early morning deliveries and knew his regular route took him through the main street of town about about five in the morning so I stood on the corner waiting for the bakery truck to come into view. Sure enough, At five o'clock I spotted the red truck coming down the street. I flagged him down and explained my predicament to him. Now, he didn't carry jumper cables in the truck so we had to go back to the bakery to retrieve a pair that were kept there for emergencies. With the cables in the truck, we headed for the lovers lane on old Roe Hook road. What a surprise when we got there, the car was not where I had abandoned it. I thought someone had run off with my brother in laws car. With my brother verbally chastising me for wasting his time and doubting my sanity, my thoughts now turned to a restauranteur with no ride home and Two angry parents I would have to face in the future.

With no alternatives left, My brother dropped me off at home and I managed to get some sleep before I gave my brother in law the news that he no longer had a car. I awoke early and called him and explained as best I could that the car was missing. After another verbal flogging, I decided I might just as well go down to his place of work and agree on a repayment plan which would take me the rest of my life knowing the limitations on my financial resources. I lived about fifteen minutes from his business and boy, that was the longest walk of my young life. Much to my surprise, when I arrived at the restaurant, parked right in front, in plain view, was the car. It was a 1951 ford sedan and it never looked so good to me.

He told me that someone had come into the restaurant at about two o'clock in the morning and told him his car was parked and abandoned on old Roe Hook road and they simply just went over, jumped the battery and drove it home. Well, everyone in the restaurant had a good laugh on me, but I was so relieved that it didn't bother me a bit. All's well that ends well, but I will never forget my experience on that night.

Richard T Vogt
June 1, 2013

15—DINERS OF OLD

November 2, 2013

I'm sitting here at the keyboard trying to decide just what I am going to write about next. That's the hardest part about being a writer, getting started. Its like trying to pull a heavy load. The initial tug on the line is about overcoming inertia. That's what the first few lines in any composition are: Literary inertia! Once that is accomplished, inertia again takes over and the words flow freely like sand in an hour glass.

Have you ever had a hamburger? I am not speaking of the gigantic piles of goop that they serve in restaurants now. I am thinking of those delicious burgers they served in the greasy spoon diners of old. Just a ground meat pattie served on a steamed roll with a slice of raw Bermuda onion on it. A little seasoning with some ketchup and a cup of hot diner coffee in a mug. You could easily eat a couple of them. Now, burgers seem to be the result of an idiotic contest to see who can produce the most outrageous example of epicurean contradiction ever known to man. They are piled so high with unnecessary ingredients that even Gatemouth Brown would have difficulty wrapping his lips around one of them. They serve them on pretzel buns, bagel buns, croissant buns and any other bun that isn't a hamburger bun.

Remember the old fashioned home fries in the diners?" Burn'em" they would call out to the short order cook and he would produce a side dish of golder brown, crunchy chunks of raw fried potatoes cooked right on the grill. Never sliced, always hand cut into pieces so that no two were alike. Deep frying was not allowed. The grill was the easel of the short order cook where he would create culinary works of art which were a pleasure for the palate. He would have a half dozen different types of food at work at one time on the grill and there was never any flavor infringement from one to the other. A huge pile of fresh cut uncooked home fries were always pushed to a corner of the grill waiting for a handful to be raked over to the greased heated surface.

The diners of old had charm and a personality all their own. Names like Orphan Annies Miss Peekskill, Sam and Bills, Swanky Franks, Sonnys, Yankee Clipper and Pat and Andys graced the entrance. Walk in a diner on a cold winter day where the windows would be all steamed up and you would be met with all the smells on the menu. Coffee, toast, hot sauce that the truckers smeared on their eggs, burgers on the grill, bacon frying. All those aromas would blend into one diner bouquet that was a treat for your sense of smell. The bleached blonde waitresses with their frilly aprons and decorative hankies pinned on their blouse would always greet you with a friendly smile. I used to drive forty miles to Sonny's Diner just to have the home fries that they served there. And if I was real lucky, I would get a seat at the counter right in front of the grill man so I could watch him work his magic on that hot metal plate where he would produce mountains of food in what seemed like minutes.

Many of the old diners were fashioned after railroad cars and usually had a sign near the entry door proclaiming "booths for ladies"

Some had the thick porcelain coffee mugs that weighed a pound and would keep the brew hot forever. It was necessary to talk above the din created by the cooks calling out for order pick ups by the waitresses, waitresses calling orders to the cook working the grill and the clanking of cups and saucers. Then on top of that, you had the juke box cranking out the latest songs on the hit parade. Conversation was ongoing as customers devoured the savory treats created for their eating pleasure. The atmosphere in a diner was sometimes carnival like where the voices and noise blended into a cacophonous concerto.

Many diners were open all night. After the drinking establishments closed, there was a parade of characters coming through the doors. Some nights you could view the dregs of humanity on display. Fist fights were a common occurrence and were usually broken up or settled quickly before either of the combatants suffered any damage other than their self respect. Most of the bands playing in the area would converge on the diners after their gig was over just to kill time. I think that people just didn't want to go home. They wanted the fun to go on forever. After a raucous night on the town it was hard to go home to an empty room with just your thoughts. Some mornings the diners would resemble a carnival freak show. Very strange people would appear. I saw a man come into a diner one night with a chimpanzee dressed in a superman outfit. The customers were dumbfounded. The guy just breezed in with him in and acted like it was the most natural thing in the world to do. He just sat this monkey down in the booth and placed an order for him just like he was a person. The chimp was just about to dig into his food when the owner convinced the man to make his order a take out. I saw a full marching band tramp right through a diner playing at the top of their lungs. Apparently their team won! I was in a crowded diner in the wee hours of the morning when the power decided to fail. Pitch black, women screaming, men laughing and yelling, pandemonium! When the power was restored after what seemed like a long time, half of the crowd was gone. (gross receipts took a dive that night) The only thing missing was the midway barker shouting his pitch "come one come all, see the greatest show on earth".

The diners of old didn't feature food selections that were favorable to the "Atkins" diet. I remember one time when I went to a diner with my wife for lunch. When she asked the waitress if they had any low cal items on the menu, she simply replied "Maa'm, nothing in this diner is low calorie". That said it all and really it was one of the many reasons for the demise of the diners of old. Heavy emphasis on obesity caused people to seek out other food emporium's with fare that coincided more closely with their dietary needs. The lifestyle of middle class America was lifted because of more readily available education which provided better paying jobs that resulted in people seeking classier venues for dining. I think people started to equate the old style diners with those living a lower class life in the class conscious society which we had evolved into. People wanted a lifestyle that more closely mimicked the way people were living in the technicolor movies they were watching. America was maturing!

I believe there are two other reasons for the decline in the number of diners. One was the migration of the population to the suburbs. There weren't people left in sufficient numbers in the urban areas to support them. Shopping malls and disorder in the urban areas caused much of the population flight to suburbia. The second reason was the massive drive by the government to build super highways. The heavy traffic was rerouted around the diners. Route sixty six is a good example of a heavily traveled highway being put out of business because of the need for faster travel. Many old diners on route sixty six just padlocked the doors because the bottom line didn't show a profit anymore. Fast food restaurants featured drive in service and to a nation on the move this was a come on. I'm sure if a poll was taken among those who frequent the fast food establishments, it would reveal the fact that most who eat there are non tippers. Some people resent tipping and think that the owners of the eating establishments should pay their workers a living wage.

I miss the diners of old. They were an oasis for the working people. You could always find some friendly conversation with people from all walks of life. People without pretension. The tattooed counterman, the short order cook, the waitresses all ready and eager to dispense their philosophy gained through years of experience. I still stop at the Village Diner in Pennsylvania and have been doing so for fifty years. This diner was built in the early forties by the Silk City diner company.

It is in remarkable condition and does a flourishing business. But it is not the diner of old. The counter grill has been moved out of sight to the back and the home fries leave a lot to be desired.

There has been a resurgence in restoring some of the old diners but I doubt they will attract the hard core "greasy spoon" die hard fans like myself. The restored models will have to comply with O.S.H.A. requirements, and new government regulations directed at eating establishments will hamper the attempt by the restorers to duplicate what was once "stylish". The disabilities act will require upgrades that will restrict the renovators progress. Just as the big bands had their era, the old greasy spoon diners have had their run. To sit in a restored diner and try and get the same feeling one got from the original would require a great stretch of the imagination. I am glad got to sit at the counter, put a nickel in the juke box, and enjoy a greasy cheeseburger in many of the grand old diners of yesteryear. Unfortunately, it is a privilege many people will never get. If that is the price of progress, then let there be no progress.

Richard T Vogt

16—SPECIAL FRIENDS

August 26, 2013

FRIENDS

Friends, we all have them. But what I want to talk about are those special friends, The ones that touch your life and seem to remain with you forever. There aren't usually a lot of them. Sometimes just a few, otherwise they wouldn't be special. I can think of a music teacher in high school, a housewife, and especially a garage mechanic who I would like to highlight in this composition.

The person I am referring to ran a service station in the small town where I lived for a major part of my life. He wasn't a religious man, but he lived his life by the golden rule. "Do unto others as you would have others do unto you", that was his credo. And through all the years I knew him, that's how he approached life every day.

He wasn't wealthy, but he had something that riches cannot buy. He loved his work. He had a mind for mechanics, for how things work. I do not believe there was anything that was broken that he couldn't fix. He could listen to an engine run and diagnose any inner workings that weren't performing properly. He didn't need computers, scopes or other technology of the modern age. He just knew. Old school!

His word was his bond, just a handshake, no written estimates or contracts. If he said he could do it, he would deliver. He was probably owed more money than anyone else in town. Most of which I doubt he ever collected. But he would still revive some old farm boys transportation even though they owed him. He was that kind of guy.

Saturday mornings were very entertaining at the garage. There would always be a few of the local characters hanging around, offering advice, kibitzing and getting in the way of progress. A local boy who ran his car at the local drag strip would bring his hot rod down for a tune up and race it up and down the road after each carburetor adjustment. This usually brought howls of approval from the assembled locals.

Friday night was a special night for him and his wife. They would drive to a Howard Johnson's restaurant for dinner and always make sure to get the same table and waitress. Sunday, they always took a ride in his corvette. They would just get in the car and drive aimlessly through the countryside enjoying the togetherness and the scenery.

He had a quick sense of humor. One day he pulled up to the local store wearing his usual blue coveralls, the same as those worn by the local veterinarian. A small boy was sitting on the steps of the store and he asked him. "Hey mister, are you the vet"? He replied "whats the matter boy, don't you feel good?" We were burning brush in his yard one day and a young boy strolling by asked if he could help. He was wearing a military camouflaged hat and said he had the complete outfit home. "You'd better not wear that boy, your mother wouldn't be able to find you" was his reply. I never saw him lose his temper. He was devoid of pretension and was always good company.

As the years piled up, he decided to sell the garage and retire. He bought a single wide trailer in Florida and became a snow bird. He and his wife enjoyed the warmth and sunshine of Florida in the winter and he was constantly trying to convince me and my wife to move down down there. After they spent a few winters in Florida, a tornado swept through their town and demolished their trailer. Luckily, they were not injured. Their neighbor was not so fortunate. I believe he was killed. Undaunted, he went ahead and had a house built in the same town. He and his wife enjoyed wintering in the house for a few years and then she got sick. After a protracted illness, she passed away. Needless to say, he was devastated. He would now have difficulty adapting to a new way of life.

About once a week, we would go out for breakfast. Usually to a different diner every time and we always ordered a Belgian waffle. I carried a bottle of liquid margarine with me to use in place of the rock hard butter served in the diners. That always got a rise out of the waitresses. He always regaled me with interesting stories about the old days and always told them in that dry humorous way that he had. Now, this was the time prior to people being infected with the "political correctness" bug so he told the stories in a much more colorful way. He would sometimes even shock me. He probably knew more about the history of the town than the town historian. Those little historical tidbits that don't ever get recorded for posterity were right at his fingertips, and most times were very amusing.

Many a cold winter night I would go to his house where we would watch the boxing matches. He had an electronic device that enabled him to pick up t v channels that I couldn't get so we enjoyed many nights of good boxing. When I would walk my German Shepard during the day, I would usually stop in his house for a visit. He always had a supply of dog biscuits on hand for my dog. She would stand in front of him until he produced one cookie and then another, ravenously devouring them. Then he would hold his hands up in the air and she would know there wouldn't be any more biscuits coming and would walk away and lay down. He got a big kick out of that. Sometimes when I would drop in, he would be finishing lunch and would put the plate on the floor and let my dog lick it clean. I'm sure his daughter would have been furious if she knew, but she never found out. I should mention that he did wash the dish afterward!

He served his country in the second world war as he served his community in peace time He accepted every challenge that confronted him with all the energy he could muster. I learned a lot about mechanics and life during the time that I knew him and we had many laughs together. I thought it was really ironic that when he died, the hearse that was parked in front of the funeral home to convey his body to the cemetery refused to start. I guess he got one last laugh. His name was Spencer Shepard, but to everyone who knew him he was just "Shep". He was my good friend and he was quite a guy!!!

Richard (Digger) Vogt

17—NEW CARITIS

November 9, 2013

There is nothing like the smell of a new car. To get behind the wheel of a new car that has never been driven is tantamount to walking in a hidden valley in the wilderness that no one has ever set foot on. I have purchased many new cars. I have found buying a new car can be a pleasant or sometimes very unpleasant experience. The selection of a new car is a very personal matter. Manufacturer, body style, cloth or leather seats. What is referred to as the "bells and whistles" of a car tell a lot about person. How a car is maintained reveals a lot about their lifestyle. When some people buy a new car for the first time, they stay with that brand of automobile for the rest of their life, sometimes even picking the same color. I have always changed the color of the cars that I buy. I have changed brands a few times, but not because of quality issues, and I have always purchased American automobiles, but now that seems not to matter much. Auto parts are manufactured all over the world and then assembled in a domestic manufacturing facility. I remember when either the Cadillac or Lincoln was the top of the line car for the high rollers, that's not the case anymore. They have taken a back seat to the imported brands.

I have purchased many new cars and would like to highlight a few of them to show just what I encountered when I entered the shadowy world of car salesmen. They are a strange breed who all appear to have attended the same school. They are baiting the hook the moment you walk in the front door. Think you are going to put one over on a car salesman? Think again!. They get up pretty early. If you are from Peoria, they've either been there or have an uncle living there." Oh, you're a veteran? So am I". They will break down your defenses or build up your ego, Whatever the situation requires." What? You want a markdown? Those days are gone forever, we only have this much to work with anymore". (then comes their forefinger and thumb a half inch apart in front of your face). Now, while you are pondering your next move, you wonder how they stay in business as you watch what seems like an army of employees wandering around the grounds. Car salesmen exude personality, they are great guys. You feel like you have just made a new friend. (without facebook) That is until you sign on the dotted line for that new piece of iron you just went into hock for. Then its "you'll have to see the service manager for that, bud".

Most of the cars I bought were just straight sales with no story attached. But a few of them were memorable. I purchased a nineteen eighty two Berlinetta (Chevrolet sports model) that was really a beauty. Burgundy with gold body striping and gold trimmed wheels. When I took the car back to the dealer for the initial five hundred mile service I was surprised while at work by a call from the service manager. She said "Mr. Vogt, we had a slight accident with your car. The sixteen foot overhead garage door came down and caved in the roof while we were bringing it into the garage for servicing. Whoa! Is this a joke? No, my car now had roof cleavage. To me, calling what happened to my new car a "slight" accident was like saying Davy Crocket and his boys had a "minor" setback at the Alamo. Well, I was given a rental and the car went into the body shop. Three days later I picked it up on a cloudy day and took that beauty home. Two days later while washing the car, I noticed what is called "Orange peel" in the surface of the paint. I took it back to the dealer and after a bit of wrangling with the service manager, It was sent back to the shop and I drove off in another rental. The second repair was not much better and the car went to a third body shop. They say the third time is the charm and it worked out that way. Car damage fixed, rental returned. Is everybody happy ? Looks that way.

Subsequently, the car was the victim of an accident where my wife was forced off the road while going to work. (more body work) Then, a few months later she was rear ended by a drunk driver while out shopping. It appeared lady luck wasn't shining down on this vehicle. We traded it in for a nineteen eighty four Firebird SE sport coupe. (good car, no problems).

We got the new car itch in nineteen eighty seven and traded the SE for a nineteen eighty seven Firebird Trans Am. Now I was always a pretty hip guy and I was dealing with a young salesman that I figured was tuned in to the times. He talked me into a car with all the goodies and I left the dealers lot happy as a lark. A few days later, we were traveling into town and I asked my wife to insert a cassette tape into the player. (compact disc players were not in cars at that time). She was fumbling around to the point where I started to get aggravated. Surprise!, There was no cd player in the car. Now it was back to the dealer where I had to verbally pummel the salesman who sold me the car without any tape player and then negotiate with the service manager (remember, the salesman isn't your buddy anymore) to have a new sound system installed in my car at an additional cost to me. Lesson learned-don't assume!

In a few years, I got tired of stuffing myself into sporty cars. It was like trying to cram ten pounds of potatoes into a five pound bag. The old bones were telling me it was time to move up to the open space of a larger car. I decided right then to aim for the top with a new Buick four door sedan. We traded the Trans Am in for a Nineteen Ninety Buick Park Avenue which was a good ride that we never had any problems with. In three years, I got the itch again and decided to move up to the big time and go out to look at the Cadillacs.

I traveled down to a neighboring town where good deals on Caddies were rumored to be the norm. The salesman was a youngster who offered me a good trade in price for the ninety Buick but would not budge on the new car price. On the way home I passed a dealership close to my house and stopped in. The salesman didn't dicker. He offered the same trade on my ninety Buick and he would discount the new Ninety three Caddie price of thirty nine thousand down to thirty thousand nine hundred dollars. As soon as my wife and I were through dancing around the floor, we were ready to sign on the dotted line. The next morning the phone rang and it was the youngster from the original dealership wanting to know if he could induce me to purchase a car from him. When I told him I bought a Caddie on the way home from my visit with him the previous day, I heard a gasp on the other end of the line. Once again, lesson learned. Once you have a nibble on the line, set the hook and reel it in quick!

I got an added bonus by purchasing the car at the local dealership. When the salesman was on his knees putting the plates on my car, I remembered him telling me that he was a retired General Motors executive moonlighting just to fill up his now idle time. I got a fiendish rush watching him perform that menial task for me. Just human nature I guess. In those days the caddie was a premier automobile. Go in for service and you were a V.I.P. It was all "cream and sugar with that sir"? And as an added bonus, I got a reaction from some of my green eyed friends and relatives that was priceless. I really enjoyed that car. In nineteen ninety seven the warranty was due to expire and I traded the Caddie for a Buick Park Avenue. Nice car no problems.

I saw my next car when my wife was doing a nursing assignment in Columbia hospital which is located in upstate New York. When picking her up at work one day, I passed a Buick dealership and there it was sitting in front of the showroom. A two thousand silver Buick Park Avenue with shiny chrome wheels and to me, it looked like a spaceship. I had to have it, it was reaching out to me. The dealer told me he could have sold a dozen of them if he had them, but he just didn't have any and couldn't seem to find one. I found it strange that the next day I went to a dealer thirty miles away in Albany New York and found just what I wanted only this one had dark tinted window glass which only made it more desirable to me. (I always liked cars with pizzaz)! When the salesman greeted me, I noticed he was laid back and used the soft sell to push cars. After the usual dickering over the price, we bought the car. Now here's where it gets a little weird. We were attending an Episcopal church in town and after the service I asked my wife if she thought the priest looked familiar. She agreed. When I went to get the car serviced a few weeks later, I inquired about the salesman that sold me my car and was told he was now an ordained priest. Apparently he was supplementing his income by selling cars. It seemed an odd way for a future man of the cloth to be earning his daily bread.

I bought a few more cars since then and have been pleased with their performance. I own a nineteen ninety four Special Edition Chevy Blazer that I bought new and after twenty years I still drive it and it looks as good as the day I bought it. It's getting so that all the cars look the same. It seems that the car designers have lost no only their imagination but also their sense of adventure. Remember the tail fins of the fifty's? The need to eliminate the reliance on fossil fuels has changed automotive design forever. Give'em some rake, get'em low, eliminate wind drag. Still don't believe in evolution? Think again.

Richard T Vogt

18—BEEKMAN DRUM CORPS

November 25, 2013

I lived in a small town in upstate New York with my former wife and three small children. The town had a population of about eighteen hundred people, but it encompassed a large area which was comprised of a dozen dairy farms. As you would expect, the residents in the town were people who toiled at some sort of manual labor for their daily bread and this was reflected in their attitudes and demeanor. Everyone knew what was happening almost before it happened. A libertarian atmosphere prevailed in their lives and just about all of the residents knew they could depend on their neighbor in times of need.

I found myself needing help when my former wife fell sick for an extended period and suddenly I was responsible not only for the upkeep of our home but also for he care of our three small children. My former wife was hospitalized for much of that time and I had a full time job that I had to report to everyday. Being in situation like this puts a person against the wall and tests their mettle. I knew that if I wanted to maintain my family, I would have to go the extra mile and dig down deep to see what I had.

There were a group of people in the town that gave me unwavering support, watching my preschool children during the day and making sure that my in school child got safely to her class every day. There were many days that they didn't want to leave the house in the morning and I had to practically drag them to the sitters house and it broke my heart, but I knew that they were in stable homes with people that would care for and protect them while I was working. These were people I could depend on and all of them had that "lean on me" attitude which made it easier to leave my children in the morning. The situation continued for months and I was thankful for the help from caring townspeople. They went out of their way to support me and enabled me to survive the situation that I found myself in. With—out their help, I doubt if I would have been able to keep my family together.

When the crisis ended, I tried to think of a way to repay the town for their kindness and support. I ruled out joining the fire company because of my experience with cliques in organizations such as this and the rivalry's that are ever present. Politics was not an option because I am strong willed and not easy to bend. So, I decided to form a fife and drum corps for the youth of the community. I would be sort of a Professor Henry Hill from River City. (The Music Man! Remember?) I played the drums all my life and was currently playing with an ancient drum corps so I was more than qualified to teach percussion.

I spoke to a representative from the fire company and he was receptive to the idea but I did notice he did not offer any support. Through word of mouth, I managed to assemble about a dozen young boys and had them come to my house every friday evening for drum lessons. This arrangement soon began to have an effect on the tranquility of my home life. Twenty four snow covered boots in the hall every Friday evening and twelve jackets scattered about the house got old pretty quick, so I negotiated the use of the local church meeting hall and classrooms for our practice sessions.

I enlisted the aid of a neighbor who played the fife and within a few weeks the drum corps started to grow. Eventually we had about twenty boys pounding the drum pads and blowing fifes every Friday night and soon it actually started to sound like a musical unit. Another fifer joined us and we were really starting to see progress. I had a parent come to the hall one night and practically begged me to let his boy join. This was after we had been practicing for about six months and the boys were showing progress. I explained to him that we were now in the advanced stages of lessons and I didn't think his boy could catch up. He assured me his boy would practice faithfully and he would see to it that he attended rehearsals regularly. I relented and came to regret it. His boy attended a few rehearsals, found it was too much like work and quit.

I found a Catholic school that had upgraded their band equipment and purchased four snare drums and two bass drums from them. I had to completely disassemble all the drums and rebuild them in the style that was popular in the sixteenth century as the corps theme would be revolutionary war. Drums in that era were held together by rope rather than steel rods as were the modern drums. I had the shells refinished with revolutionary war insignias painted on them and they looked authentic. I cajoled the ladies auxiliary into sewing uniforms for the entire corp which numbered about twenty and they did a good job. I was able to purchase tri-cornered hats that were typically worn by corps of this type and with the addition of jabots sewn by the ladies, they looked like midget minute men.

Teaching them to march like a military unit was difficult to do. I would march them around the school parking lot until their feet were sore. I was intent on putting a unit on the street that was as close to military precision as kids can be, and good enough was not enough for me. I told them we wouldn't appear in public until they were moderately proficient on their instruments. They all put their shoulder to the wheel and I finally had a unit that I felt was ready to be sent out to the parade circuit.

Our first parade was a County Fair parade where we marched in front of the local firemen. Myself and the two fife instructors marched with the boys which helped fill out the drum corps.

My daughter was the majorette and my son was in the color guard. When we got to our stepping off point at the parade, I told everyone that they were responsible for the care of their instruments and uniforms and they should bring them to the next rehearsal. The parade went well and the new drum corps made a very good showing. The music was acceptable and they managed to stay in both step and formation. There is usually a mob scene following a parade with everyone crowding around and fire trucks trying to work their way through the crowd to return to their duty stations. I told the kids before the parade to hold on to their instruments and hats in all this confusion.

The following week, one of the drummers came prancing in to rehearsal without his drum. When I asked him where it was, he gave me that deer in the headlights look and I knew it was lost. I called the Sheriffs Department and the fair grounds security staff but no luck. I often wonder if that person who stole the drum had any feelings of remorse when he looked at the stolen drum in his house. Probably not!

One night a local drummer walked into our rehearsal hall and started showing his proficiency with a pair of sticks and demonstrating a different drumming technique that I did not use. Well, I made him understand that he was as welcome at our rehearsals as a pork roast at a Bar Mitzva. Usually those kind of people don't hang around long at any event. They come in, make a splash, and before the ripples subside, they disappear.

I kept the corps going for about four years and then, because of lack of interest by the community, I relinquished the leadership and the fife instructor took over. The corps lasted for a couple of more years and then disbanded. It is difficult to keep any youth oriented group going forever. The kids lose interest in any repetitious routine. They expect new things in life, which they should. The parade season was during the summer and that's when young boys want to be playing baseball and doing all those "summer" things that they do. I enjoyed the time I spent with them and seeing them develop into musicians. I don't know if any of them pursued music later in life, but if they did, I liked to think that maybe I planted that musical seed in their minds that never left them.

Richard T Vogt

19—THOSE MARVELOUS MODEL A'S

October 21, 2013

Have you ever ridden in a Model A Ford? If not, rush right out and find someone that owns one and take a ride. They were really mechanical wonders. They were manufactured from nineteen twenty eight to nineteen thirty one and ford built five million of them. The four cylinder engine produced forty horsepower and the top speed was sixty five miles an hour, (though not recommended) I owned two of them. The first one was a 1930 tudor sedan that I bought from a farmer who owned an apple orchard. When I went to pick up the car I noticed all kinds of commercial ford signs around the various buildings on the property and someone later told me the farmer was once the local authorized Ford dealer.

There is not another sound that compares to the sound of a Model A Ford when the engine is idling. You can hear the individual cylinders firing with with a sort of clickety ping that is soothing to the ear. They were built high so that they could maneuver the rough roads that were so common in those years. They had shock absorbers but most of the time they weren't hooked to the frame because they just didn't absorb the shock too well. A single vacuum powered wiper blade about six inches in length was used to provide clear vision in inclement weather. These wipers didn't work too well on hills because the engine lost vacuum when laboring. Doesn't sound too good does it? But boy, were they fun to drive around. They were more fun than having a monkey in the house!

They had a manifold heater that was simply a jacket surrounding the exhaust manifold that would transfer the exhaust heat from the engine to the passenger compartment. The amount of heat sent out was determined by a flapper on the firewall. They not only were hard to control, they could be dangerous in case of a manifold leak.

The klaxon or oooga horn was one of the features most people liked about the car. It had a sound that was never reproduced by any other car maker. Most owners didn't know it, but it was possible to pull up on the gear shifter when the car was at cruising speed and push the shifter rod up against the dashboard to provide more room in the front seat. The gas tank was located right in front of the windshield and the gas was fed to the engine by gravity. There was a petcock located beneath the dash so that the tank could be shut off when the car wasn't being used. This prevented flooding of the carburetor. I can recall a funny incident with the car when I was building an extension on my home. The contractor I hired asked if he could take the Model A to pick up some material that he needed. Knowing that he was a southern boy, I figured he was familiar with Model A's and in fact I figured he had hauled moonshine using them a few times knowing what I did about his background. Well, he drove away and about fifteen minutes later the phone rang. It was Frank telling me that the car quit running and wouldn't start. I almost hated to ask the next question which was "did you open the petcock"? I could just about see his face getting red over the phone. I worked at a local manufacturing plant and used to take it to work on occasion. There was One day that I took it and a surprise snow squall struck just as we were getting out of work. With a vertical windshield and a Six inch wiper blade powered by vacuum, I knew I might have to put Jesus up on the dashboard. When the road was level, no problem. But I had to go up a steep hill after leaving the plant and that's when the trouble started. When I started the climb, the wipers couldn't push the heavy snow off the windshield and that's when I rolled down the window and started to give the wiper arm a manual assist. Wouldn't you know it, the wiper arm broke off in my hand. Here I am in pretty heavy traffic with wet snow slamming down on the windshield and I cant see in front of me. I stuck my head out the window and with snow now slamming me in the face, I somehow reached my turn off the main road. It's ha ha now looking back, but it wasn't then. Then the snow miraculously turned to rain and I put Jesus back in my pocket.

It was surprising to me how people responded to the car. I got a phone call one day from a man I didn't know. He told me that he was the construction foreman on a new interstate highway that was being built that would go through our area. He told me he was renting a house down the road and noticed the Model A in my driveway, and It seems he always had the desire to ride in one and never got the chance. I invited him over and not only took him for a ride, but I let him drive it for a few miles. He couldn't stop thanking me, a childhood wish had been fulfilled. I hope that he went out and purchased one after that, but I never knew. Older people would always tell me of their experiences with Model A's and it would always draw a crowd in a parking lot.

A good friend of mine got bitten by the bug and just had to have a Model A. We located one about fifteen miles from his house and decided to go look at it. It was a 1931 pick up truck that had been parked out in a wooded lot exposed to the elements for a few years and was in pretty rough condition although it was sound. It had a fender just hanging on with a few bolts and the roof material was in shreds. It had two flat tires and the windshield was missing. Oh! and one door wouldn't stay shut. Despite all its shortcomings, my buddy fell in love with it and after some haggling, a price was agreed on. We fixed the flats, tied the door shut and hoped the fender would stay with the car on the trip to his house. I offered to tow it, but my buddy was eager to give it a road test. (In those days, we didn't worry about little things like license plates and no fault insurance.)

It started on the first try and we were on our way over the back roads to his house. Talk about the Beverly Hillbilly's, this truck made them look sophisticated. It was splattered with mud and the rear fender was bouncing around like a basset hounds ear. I was laughing so hard I could hardly keep up with him. About halfway home, the fender came flying off the truck and I just stopped, picked it up and threw it in the bed of the pick-up. It only heated up once on the way home and when it did, it looked like a Stanley Steamer. Well, my buddy fixed it up real nice and had many, many happy times with that truck.

My second Model A was a 1929 pick up truck. I was approached one day by a co worker who knew someone wanting to sell the truck. He had a photo and it was parked in an apple orchard with apples all over it. I made an offer which he refused, only to contact me a year later to agree on the original price. Now I would have to transport it to my house which was about thirty miles away. I got my other Model A buddy and he agreed to help me tow it home. I had a nineteen fifty three Ford Sedan which I would use as a tow car. We started out early in the morning on a cold November day with a tow chain and an old tire. We managed to remove most of the apples from the truck and got it hooked up for the long tow. It was so cold that we agreed that whoever was maneuvering the truck would wear two jackets and that when the cold became unbearable, we would switch drivers in the truck. (this occurred frequently) We were coming through one of the towns on the route and there was a cop sitting in a car alongside the road. As we slowly eased past the car, we noticed that the cop was fast asleep, lucky for us!.

We parked the truck in my yard and commenced cleaning out the rest of the apples and other debris when a chipmunk darted out from under the seat. Scared the heck out of both of us. I timed the engine, put some gas in the tank and it kicked right over. The previous owner told me that it hasn't been started in five years. I was in the process of rehabilitating the vehicle when a young guy stopped in to look at it and wanted to buy it. All I did was repack the water pump, fix the roof and clean it up a little. I was using it to ride around the fields in back of my house and having a great time with it, but I had four cars registered and on the road so it didn't make sense to try and restore this one. The young fellow was coming back on a regular basis to try and get me to part with the truck. He was almost to the point of being obsessed with owning the truck. He struck me as a guy who would really do a good resto job on it so I made him an offer that I thought he would refuse. He agreed on the price to my surprise. It was more than ten times what I paid for the vehicle. When he came to tow it home, it was getting dark so I gave him an old railroad kerosene lantern to tie on the back of it. He even returned the lantern the following week. I finally sold my nineteen thirty sedan to another Model A aficionado and he did a complete resto on it and It is still running and registered to this day. (although owned by yet another person) Henry Ford opened up a new world with his Tin Lizzie and then the "A". He was both a mechanical genius and a manufacturing innovator who changed america for the better.

Richard T Vogt

20—THE MYSTERIOUS PLANE CRASH

6-22-2013

Most of my working life was spent working for a giant corporation and to get to my place of work, I had to travel Thirty miles. To alleviate the everyday stress of driving and the monotony of aloneness while driving, I joined a car pool with four other commuters. We worked the night shift and had to travel on what was at one time the main route going north in the state. It, like many other highways was rendered a secondary road by a new thruway which had been built to the west of it so the traffic was always light, especially at night.

Joe was one member of the car pool and he had the uncanny ability to always be around when something unusual or exciting took place. He would be sitting in a diner having lunch and the place would get held up. A wheel would fall from an airplane and where would it land ? Why, in Joes backyard. A pizza delivery vehicle collides with a live poultry truck at an intersection, chickens running all over the road and there's Joe, just standing on the corner. Well, anyway, it was Joe's turn behind the wheel this particular night and we were all eager to get home from work. As we sped down the darkened highway, there was the usual chatter from the other members of the car pool. As we came around a bend in the road, Joe shouted "Wow, that plane is really low" apparently he saw a plane flying between the two small mountains on either side of the road. As we rounded the bend he yelled "Look it crashed" The rest of us looked out and saw roaring flames on the side of the mountain. We all panicked at the same time. There were no cell phones so we figured we would speed down the road, get stopped by a police officer and report the crash. Well, we got to the next town without getting pulled over and went into the police station to report what we saw. They took our names and we went home to bed.

About 3:00 am, my phone rang and Joe asked me if I would ride up to the crash site with him and the state troopers who were coming to pick him up. I got dressed and drove to his house where Two young troopers were waiting for us. It was about fifteen miles to the site and it was drizzling. Those troopers gave us an express ride up the highway. They drove up into the mountain along narrow dirt roads for an hour or so but we found no evidence of a plane. Then they called in reinforcements and about Three more troop cars arrived. Now it was getting serious. The captain in charge of the investigation told us that if we couldn't find any traces of the plane on the ground he would call a helicopter out from The local airport. About that time, a fire truck and an ambulance pulled up and parked at the side of the road. This was now a major recovery effort. It was getting serious and I was starting to get a little weak kneed. After all, only Joe actually saw the plane. I just saw some flames on the hillside. I never saw a plane. I started to question why we were there. The mosquitos were out in full force and I had welts all over my face and neck from their bites. On top of that it was still hot and humid at 6:00 am in the morning. I was ready to call it a day. With troop cars scouring the hills for wreckage, we sat and waited. Now with all these official vehicles flashing their lights, it looked like the invasion of the body snatchers. And of course this caused a lot of rubbernecking along the highway which resulted in a traffic jam from the early morning commuters on their way to work. All this started to have an effect on the captain in charge which caused him to start getting a little edgy which in turn brought renewed questioning about just what we thought we saw. A call came in from one of the troopers searching up in the hills that he found that the town dump was still smoldering from a recent burn. At that point, the captain in charge decide that we were on a mission impossible and called all the troop cars in. He thanked us for being vigilant and for staying up to aid in the search and that was that.

The next day, the local newspaper ran the headline "PLANE HUNT CALLED OFF" and had a full page story of the incident. Well, my home phone was ringing off the hook all day long until I went to work at 3:00 in the afternoon. I got calls like "is Hop Harrigan there?" Or the one that got a lot of play "when does the next plane leave for the dump"? When I arrived for work at the plant, they were ready. Our co-workers rode us like a new bicycle. They were unrelenting in their mockery and good natured taunts. We took it all in stride every night without let up and then about a month later we struck back at our tormenters. Our plan for revenge was unique, hilarious and executed with precision. Our ride home at night was about thirty miles and there was one car load of co workers who really razzed us at every chance they got when they would pass us on the way. We devise a ruse to get our revenge. We tolerated their daily catcalls on the way home for about a month and then one night we made sure to leave early to be on the road ahead of them. When we came to to an overpass to a creek we pulled our car askew of the road and stood on the bridge until we saw their car approaching in the distance. Then we peered over the edge of the bridge looking down at the water. They stopped and asked, "whats the matter? Do you see a plane down there"? We responded, "A car went off the road and there are two people trapped in the submerged car". Their doors flung open and they came running toward the bridge and that's when we busted out laughing and ran to our car leaving them standing there with their mouths agape. Ahhh! Revenge is sweet. They didn't razz us after that.

Richard T Vogt

21—THE PARK STREET LANES

6-10-2013

I went bowling last week with a few friends. It was the first time I had been bowling in at least 60 years. I was amazed at the changes that have taken place within the bowling alleys. They now have arcade rooms where one can be occupied with robotic electric games (for a price) restaurants that serve sushi, baby sitting services for the little ones, electronic scorekeeping, and some even have a dress code for the evening hours.

My, how times have changed. When I was a teenager, over 60 years ago, I was a pin-boy at the Park Street bowling alleys in Peekskill NY. The business had just ten alleys. eight of the alleys were for the use of regular bowling and the remaining two were used for the game of either duck pins or candlestick bowling. Duck pins were shaped like regular bowling pins except that they were about half the size and had a rubber bumper ring around the center of the pin. Candlesticks were just about what the name implied, candle shaped pins about three inches in diameter and about 16 inches tall. In both cases, twenty pins were used to play the game. The ball used to scatter the pins was different from a regular bowling ball in that it was about one third the size of a regular ball and did not have any finger holes drilled into it. The player merely cupped the ball in his hand and let it fly down the alley. Pinboys were reluctant to work the alleys for this type of bowling because there were no steel rods to locate the pins on and because the pins would really scatter and fly around when hit by the ball and could cause injury to anyone in the immediate vicinity. The candlestick pins would sometimes splinter and send forth sharp pieces of wood that could be dangerous to anyone nearby. After the bowler knocked down the pins, (regular bowling) the pinboy put them back to their proper location. He did this by depressing a mechanical lever which sent steel half inch rods up through holes in the alley. He then placed the bowling pins (which had holes in the bottom of the pins) on the protruding rods. And heaven help the pinboy who did not have the pins in the right location. (hey! spot that no. 7 or 3 pin, kid) was heard often. The pit was a dangerous place to be with pins flying every which way when they were struck by the bowling ball. We usually tended to two alleys (called jumping). There was a partition between the two alleys and the pinboy would straddle the partition and lift his legs up when the bowler threw the ball to prevent any flying pins from hitting him.

The ball return system sent the ball back to the bowler by an above the floor gutter and people would stand outside the building for hours looking through the wire covered windows at the balls rolling in both directions. It didn't take much to entertain people in those days. Some would stand there for hours. There were signs posted all over the premises which loudly declared "DONT LOFT THE BALL" that meant not to throw the ball in an arc so that it would hit the alley with a thud. That was strictly verboten! And anyone doing so was quickly taken to task by the person closest to them. The alleys were strictly for bowling. There was no food of any kind available except for a few bags of potato chips and a bottle of soda. (usually Coke or Nehi beverages). The manager on duty usually had a small radio in his cubicle to satisfy his own appetite for music or to catch up on the latest news. He also handed out bowling shoes to those amateurs not having their own personal shoes. (The red flag went up for those people and they were scrutinized to make sure no lofting of the ball took place.) When the various organizations in town had a league bowling night, the bar next door would really cash in. There would be a constant stream of people going next door and coming back with trays of beer. The beer really flowed. Just about everyone smoked back then and and there was no air conditioning so the entire place was a cloud of smoke. The din could be overwhelming on busy nights. It was hard, sweaty work setting up pins and there was alot of "hanging around" time on slow nights, but the money made it all worthwhile. The more the beer flowed, the better the tips for the pinboys.

Rchard T Vogt

22—WELL, NOW

DECEMBER 24, 2013

Of all the incidents I have experienced in my life, this one probably was the one that I would put in the "close shave" column. I was preparing to go into the local town with one of my students from a drum class that I was teaching to assist him in selecting a new drum practice pad. I told him it would be a hurry up trip because of all the projects that I had going on around my house. At the time, I was building a new addition to my house that was a two car garage. I had remodeled my my former garage into a beautiful great room and needed protection from the elements for my autos. I was also building a new patio behind the garage which necessitated my building a stone wall to terrace the spot where the patio would be located.

While driving along the road into town, I spotted a stone wall parallel to the road and couldn't resist stopping to see if I could collect a few stones for my wall. This was some-thing I was constantly doing, throwing stones in my car whenever I found one or a few. While examining the the stone wall, I noticed what looked like an old stone foundation from a building that had long since given way to the ravages of the severe northern climate. I walked into the brush and sure enough, there were stones in the foundation that I could use. As I was walking around the foundation with my student tagging along behind me the ground suddenly gave way and I plummeted straight down into a deep hole. Luckily, I fell straight down, just brushing the sides of the hole with my shoulders (it's not the fall, but the sudden stop that hurts).

As I peered upward, I could see that I had fallen into an old abandoned well that had dried up many years ago. I was shaken, but not hurt. It looked to me that the well was abut ten or twelve feet deep and had perfectly straight walls. Who ever dug the well probably a hundred years ago did a good job. There was some debris on the bottom with what looked like the skins of some snakes that had slithered into the pit over the years,. and were trapped like I was (fortunately I planned on leaving, they didn't). The student that was with me started to panic, but I told him to go back to the road and flag down a car for some assistance. As I looked up, I could see that the top four feet of the hole was lined with stones to prevent a cave in when the ground softened in the spring. Its funny, but I saw them as possible candidates for my wall at home. I could see that some rotten boards had fallen in with me and surmised that someone had covered the well and the boards were just rotting and covered with leaves and branches which accounted for me not spotting the well. There was some vine type vegetation growing out of the sides of the wall which was reminiscent of a scene from a horror movie.

After what seemed like an eternity, I heard movement at the top of the hole. When I looked up, I saw two nuns dressed in full habit peering down into the hole. Now the impact of landing and the thin foul air at the bottom of the well made me a little light headed and when I saw the nuns, I figured that even though I wasn't Catholic, the fall killed me and I was channeled up to heaven where the nuns were the guardians of the lofty domain and were looking me over. When one of them spoke to me, I was relieved. I asked them to try to summon help from a passing motorist. One of them left and one stayed with me calling out words of encouragement. In a short time the nun returned with a man who was more nervous than I was. He wanted the nuns to hold onto his ankles while he hung over the edge to grab my hands. I nixed that idea because I thought his weight would dislodge the rocks on the top of the well and they would come crashing down on me.

I think it is important to note that cell phones were not in use by the public at that time and there were no first responders ready to spring into action to render aid to those in distress. So I knew that any help that arrived would be sporadic and and by pure luck. The road was a secondary route seldom used by everyday drivers and not everyone would be inquisitive enough to stop. I figured I was in for a long wait.

By now I had determined that the nuns were probably from the house down the road where they resided.

As more people arrived, I could hear the conversations taking place above me. I told the man peering down the hole to keep every one at least ten feet from the edge to prevent a cave in. Finally through the blur of conversation a man asked if I thought I could hang on to a rope if one was lowered. I didn't think that in my dehydrated state it would be possible. Then, someone told me that a painting contractor had stopped and was bringing an extension ladder to the site to extricate me from my predicament. When he arrived, he very carefully lowered the ladder down the hole and I commenced the climb out of the well. I climbed slowly up the ladder bracing my back against the dirt wall for support. It was a short climb, but in the condition I was in, it was a hard few feet. I could see as I neared the top of the hole that a considerable crowd had gathered to see what was going on. As I emerged, a cheer erupted from the crowd and I was very happy to see the sun.

Among the crowd was the owner of the property on which the well was located. I remember him because he had a consumptive cough and a beard full of breakfast. He was lecturing someone within earshot of the principles of eminent domain and when he saw me, he approached and demanded to know what I was doing on his property. I sensed that this man had an attitude that I had to destroy very quickly. I told him That I was experiencing severe pain in my legs and back which he could see was leading up to the term "liability". Now that is a word that you don't want to hear if you are a property owner on whose property someone has just been injured. Like magic, his attitude changed. He was now very sympathetic to my needs. He told me that the hole would be filled in immediately and that the land was being developed for housing.

Finally, a local policeman arrived on the scene and interviewed me and the property owner. I refused medical attention, telling the officer that I would go to my own doctor to be checked out. The policeman told the owner to cover the hole immediately and that led to a stroke of good luck for me. I told him I was driving a station wagon in which

I could fit a panel of plywood. I offered to drive down the road to a lumber yard and obtain a piece for him. I went down, got the plywood and he compensated me generously for the trip. After a few heavy boulders were placed on top of the plywood, the hole was secured. And so ends the saga of my trip almost to the center of the earth!

RICHARD T VOGT

23—MEDIOCRITY

December 3, 2013

I sometimes wonder where we are headed as a country. I'm constantly offended by the way our values have eroded over the years. Remember when a handshake was as good as a legal contract? When someone gave you their word and staked their reputation on it? Those days disappeared many years ago. Where did we get off the track? What happened? Seventy percent of the people in the country don't trust anyone anymore. I think the blame for that should be placed on the shoulders of our elected officials. They lie and whats more, they profit from it. If a politician told the truth when he or she were campaigning, they would be defeated every time they ran for office.

I'm not one to demand perfection in everything I see or do, but c'mon, try a little harder and be a little more demanding. Have you gone to a concert or a play lately? Me and my wife attend many of them and I sit and wonder and also get very annoyed at the behavior of the audience at the end of a performance. Even though the performers are mediocre, they receive a standing ovation. It doesn't just happen randomly anymore It seems to be the rule rather the the exception. By what standard does the audience measure the quality of the performance? Is it political correctness run amok? Similar to all the little league players getting a trophy so no one has their self esteem bruised. To me it seems to be the case. I am rarely disappointed by the quality of the music or the performers for that matter. But are they always deserving of a standing ovation? I think not. But it seems there is always some doofus up in the front of the audience who can't wait to jump up an applaud. It seems that they are on the edge of their seat hoping to be the first to spring up like a Jack In The Box to lead their followers in a rousing cheer for an unearned honor. Yes, I believe a standing ovation should be reserved for those performances that are once in a lifetime occurrences. Of course, when the doofus stands up, the lemmings follow. One by one they rise until the entire audience is on their feet. Most of them just don't want to feel foolish sitting and looking at someone's back side.

There are many performers who I have admired over the years who excel in their profession that would get a standing ovation from me based not only on their performance but on their staying power through the years. Frank Sinatra, Sarah Vaughn, and Elvis Presley would all qualify because they had once in a lifetime voices. The Rolling Stones, not for the quality of their music but for their ability to endure over the years, and Evil Knievel strictly for his daring to perform feats some people didn't even have the courage to watch. I could go on and on, but I believe I made my point. They refer to some of these young rock singers as Diva's. When I was young the only singer I ever heard referred to as a Diva was Maria Callas, the opera singer. It was a term used only for really special, over the top performers.

Mediocrity has crept into our lives and we seem to accept it without question. The food in many restaurants today is mediocre and people will go into these places, devour the food at inflated prices and leave satisfied. It is rare that a salad will contain anything but arugula and lettuce anymore. Tomatoes are as rare in a salad today as a Mormon at a klan rally. But go out to eat and you had better bring something to read while waiting for a table. People have accepted mediocrity as the norm today. I used to patronize a local sandwich shop until I noticed the chicken sandwiches were nothing but lettuce and pepper sandwiches. When I contacted their headquarters about this, I never even got a response. It was like "If you don't eat it, someone else will" I don't know where all the chefs are that graduate from the C.I.A. (Culinary Institute of America)are. I suppose they are all employed at the high end restaurants where most people cant afford to go.

Entertainment in music today is to the listener like a light lunch of crackers and Brie. The appetite has not been quelled. There is still a hunger for more. More variation, more fullness, more quality. The electric guitar has hurt music more than it has helped it. Today it is not uncommon to see a band made up of five guitars and a drummer. No brass, no reeds to fill in the holes in the music that stick out like a Shetland pony in a Saratoga post parade. The guitars attempt to simulate the sounds made by the horns, but it just doesn't work. Most bands are made up of three chord musicians while garage bands masquerade as headliners in a crowded field where they perform for tin ears and get rich in the bargain. There is that old bugaboo again, mediocrity, rearing it's ugly head. Clubs will advertise "live music" and surprise you with just a Jimmy Buffet look alike playing tired out beach songs. Ho hum! For the smaller venues like weddings and local parties, the small combo's have been replaced by the Dee Jay. Now there is a fine example of musical retrograde. Why not just plug in a juke box? The dj's are usually so loud that conversation is impossible in the audience. All of the music today is played with pumped up volume and most singers have tonal qualities that rank down there with Tiny Tim. (remember him)? But the voice isn't important, the vocalists usually can't be heard above the din. Classic Hank Williams country music has been replaced by something called rockabilly, which is akin to southern dixie music with a nasal twang. The drums are amplified in most rock bands today and the drummer is seated behind a plexiglass wall that separates him from the band to provide volume control (Or maybe flying bottles). Most rock concerts today are more like pyrotechnic exhibitions than musical presentations. And when do they retire? Some of the musicians today look like they are on leave from a nursing home.

Television entertainment has bowed to mediocrity. Comedy shows of today cry out for creative writers but can't seem to find them. Comedians can't seem to get a laugh unless they talk about body parts or functions or maybe even ridicule those more pathetic than themselves. They can't keep it clean. Some of them make Lenny Bruce look like an alter boy. Comedy shows that were hilariously funny many years ago have been rekindled and hardly rate a chuckle from today's audience. In an effort to build up a following, one show features people attempting to do dangerous stunts which most of the time end with disastrous results. People finding humor in other peoples pain is unsettling and portends a fading of civility. One popular show has daily fistfights between guests who are appearing on the show for the purpose of trying to straighten out their current unbearable life, yet it continues to deteriorate on camera to the delight of the audience. The morning shows will fly someone in from Osh Kosh just to talk about a potato chip the person found in a bag that they say looks like Jesus. And they will sit there and discuss it for an hour. They will bring on a culinary expert weighing three hundred pounds and have him make some fat free hamburgers and then feature an electronics expert to demonstrate the latest in electronic gadgetry developed to allow the viewer more leisure time for television viewing such as the boring show they are currently watching. Mediocrity at its finest!

The television news shows scramble to attract a following for their twenty four hour coverage by looping the same castrophy and droning on about some child that was denied the right to sell lemonade from her front yard. They parade a cavalcade of beauties on the screen as station consultants who rave (usually all at once) in answer to a predetermined set of questions presented by the host for which they have prepared answers. (most of the ladies are attorneys, can't they find a job in the legal field?). When an incident of national significance occurs, the anchor men are as happy as a politician at a liars club meeting and pounce on it like a hungry lion. Facts are not important, just get a story out to the masses. The result is mediocre reporting.

Have you flown lately? Unwashed passengers, cramped seats, a charge for overhead storage, and peanuts for lunch. Are you satisfied with the education your child is getting in the public school system? Getting tired of having conversations with robotic voices when seeking help for an appliance that was made in Taiwan? I suppose you should be thankful you can at least understand the robot. You could be talking to Bangla Desh. No, things aren't what they used to be and they never will be again, get used to it. Its all being done to satisfy the bottom line, people aren't part of the equation anymore. You will learn to love mediocre, you will evolve!

Richard T Vogt

24—STRIKE UP THE BAND

July 22, 2013

I have been involved with music for most of my life. It started when I took drum lessons in junior high school. I bought a pair of drumsticks, a drum pad and I was on my way. My teacher was a man named Ed Shulman and he was a great guy. I caught onto drumming quickly and I think it was because Mr Shulman was an excellent percussionist and that I had an inborn flair for rhythm and coordination. My progress was so rapid that I was enlisted as a member of the high school band where I eventually became line drum captain.

My next experience with drumming happened when I enlisted in the navy at the start of the Korean war. After enlisting, I was sent to boot camp for training which would last twelve weeks.

The first week of boot training I saw a notice on the bulletin board that musicians were needed to fill out the training base drum and bugle corps. The base drum and bugle corps performed at all base functions such as graduation ceremonies, dedications, and holiday events. I was reluctant to audition at first because I thought that with a pool of sailors from all over the east coast, the competition would be too severe. But I found that all drum corps members were exempt from the grueling Saturday morning inspections of the barracks and just hearing that was reason enough for me to go and try out for the drum line. When I arrived at the base office for the audition, the chief petty officer in charge asked me the routine questions about my training and experience. I guess I didn't exhibit much confidence in myself when I told him that high school drumming was all I had in my repertoire. Well, that didn't faze him. He handed me a pair of drumsticks, pointed to a drum pad on the long table and said "lets see what you can do" I ran down the few rudiments that I knew and then went through a fancy six eight maneuver and stood there waiting for his decision. He looked at me and said "boy, you're the best damn drummer I got" I felt good! I played at many ceremonies before I graduated from boot training and really enjoyed it.

After being discharged from the navy I got married and bought a set of trap drums (drums used in bands and orchestras). I would throw the drums in the car on a Saturday night and play anywhere a drummer was needed and sometimes where a drummer wasn't needed. I used to go to a bar where they had an accordion player doing a solo gig and set up and play along with him. He was more than happy to see me come in. The only problem was that he got paid and I didn't. That bar was the kind of place where anything goes. Rowdy, but a lot of fun. One night a stranger came in with a metal washtub, a piece of board and a length of rope which he transformed into a bass that he called a devils bass. Much to our surprise, he was getting the notes we needed from that contraption and it was a big hit with the lets have a good time Saturday night crowd.

I then joined a combination fife and drum corps that specialized in civil war music and wore west point cadet uniforms. They were suffocating in the hot weather and doubled in weight when they got wet in a parade. (which happened often). I was also playing in a dance trio at the time which was my first play for pay gig (I was on my way to the big time). I stayed with the trio for awhile and then got into a band playing at the local germania club. While still in the drum corps, I continued playing German music at the hall where it seemed that the people would dance to music of different tempos with ease. Waltz and march tempos were much in demand. When the schnops was flowing, the rhinelanders burned up the dance floor. I still remember the delicious food that they served there. Two of the band members were about my age and we would get a bit jazzy at times. Then, the old guard at the club would let us know that that type music was verboten! Needless to say, sweet georgia brown won out over the jolly coppersmith and the three of us parted company with the protectors of the fatherland to start a dixieland band.

I was still drumming with the corps and after a parade ended, we would go to the bull pen (a big field or parking lot) where the fireman would commence to drain all the beer kegs and the drum corps would play till the wee hours of the morning. At one of these sessions I noticed a revolutionary war type corps (known as ancient corps) and the type drumming they were doing. I was taken by it, I wanted to drum like that. I approached a member of the corps drum line and asked if they needed drummers. (that's like asking billy graham if he needs any more converts). I studied rudimental drumming for Two years and in the meantime left the corps I was with to join the ancient corps. All of the drummers in the ancient corps were soldiers at West Point and played with the army band stationed there. The three of us who left the germania club formed a six piece dixieland band and named it "the bridge city six" which was the nickname of the city in which we played. I remember playing in a roadhouse on a Saturday night for ten dollars each and all the pizza we could eat. We traveled to Schenectady on a Saturday night in February for twelve dollars each. Driving back, we ran into freezing rain and didn't get home until eight o'clock in the morning. Dixieland music was fun to play, but its appeal was limited to a select group of people. I should mention here that money wasn't always the motivator when playing music. I knew an older musician who told me that in the forties, musicians used to make a dollar fifty for a four hour gig and that sometimes a band member would be lured to another band for an additional twenty five cents. I had a full time job and didn't rely on music to sustain me. Most of the musicians I knew were in the same situation. We did it for the love of music.

When the Dixie beat got stale, I moved on to country music with a group called the "Sundowners". I was really not content with the music they were playing as it was the old style country and not much of a challenge for a drummer. A guitar player called me and told me that a band that played in a bottle club was looking for a drummer. A bottle club is simply a place that doesn't have a license to sell alcohol so they allow the customers to bring their own and the establishment provides the set-ups for a price. So I joined a band called The "countrymen" and played, you guessed it, country music. The leader, Ginny Mae, was one of the best female country singers I ever backed. They would have jam sessions on Sunday afternoons that would draw hundreds of people. They always had security guards on duty at these events to keep the cowboys in line and minimize the incidence of flying missiles. It was while I was with this band that I started filling in occasionally on vocals. The band leaders husband Bill, would always make a batch of hot dogs and sauerkraut on Saturday nights and although they were delicious, the place smelled like the mens room at the Yale bowl during a preseason football game. But, alcohol does have a a tendency to dull the senses and no one ever complained. Now, Ginny had an appetite for men that unfortunately extended to band members. She wasn't the type that would arouse a young mans fancy and I wasn't in the market for divorce proceedings so I left the band along with one of the guitar players and formed a dance band that played pop tunes and standards which were more in demand from the audience I was looking for.

About that time I found out that the West Point drummers in the ancient corp were getting paid for each parade we marched in while other members were not. When I took my grievance to the leader of the corps, they offered to pay me also, but not the other members. I left that corps and joined another ancient corps in connecticut. I should note here that I received no compensation for marching in parades. It took up a lot of my time and was and expense to me. I would get home from work, sometimes not even eat supper, pile the wife and kids in the car and drive thirty miles to march in a parade. During the summer months, this was a weekly happening. All of the parades were firemanic with the boys in blue showing off their equipment and vying for trophys. I did march down fifth avenue in the big apple once to commemorate Puerto Rico day although I never did get the connection there.

It was about this time that I played musical chairs, switched wives and assembled a four piece band with a guitar play who did vocals. The bass player and the lead guitar player were constantly at odds with one another. They bickered about everything. The lead guitar player was sort of a prima donna and knew that without vocals, we weren't marketable. We played a gig at a firehouse and they held us over for an hour and then it was another hour holdover and we were pretty tired. Someone in the audience requested a song that wasn't in our repertoire and then decided to grab the guitar off the stand after we wouldn't try to play it. The lead guitar player punched the guy and a fight broke out. (the only time it happened in all the years I played.) Needless to say that was sort of the proverbial straw so we broke up the band after a new years eve gig.

I filled in with a trumpet player who actually didn't have a band but had cards printed up and would book gigs for weddings, parties and such. He would find out from the client just how big a band they wanted and then would round up the musicians he would need. I sat in with him for a year and don't recall ever playing with the same people. I was really taken by surprise when we assembled one night to play a party, to see a man from my old neighborhood who used to teach music from his house when I was just a kid. He was the rhythm guitar player for the night. He was as equally surprised to see me. At the same time, I was working with a guy from Germany who played an accordion and would book small parties. He was at one time a star on German TV and was quite good. He eventually bought a cordovox with a cheater (built in rhythm feature) and didn't need the beat of a live drummer after that. I did meet up with him a short time later and he told me that it wasn't as much fun playing solo, but the money was better. (das kapitalist!!!). The next band was a five piece band (Kansas City) with a male vocalist that didn't play an instrument. He owned a diner and we would practice at the diner after closing and drink the stale coffee. He was another prima donna and I was beginning to suspect that it was a flaw that afflicted all male vocalists. When I would do a vocal, he couldn't hide his annoyance. But no vocalist can perform every song well and we played to please the crowd. We were together about three years and developed a pretty good sound. We booked a gig in a bar called the "Country Gentlemen" which was located right next to the "No-Tel Motel". When the night was over the owner gave us a bonus for drawing a crowd big of big spenders and booked us the following saturday night. The base player and vocalist decided that they couldn't make it as they had other commitments. We didn't want to lose a gig that presented such lucrative possibilities so we located a singing bass player from another band who was free that night and asked him to sit in with us. We had another successful night. This didn't go over well with our bass player and vocalist. (Ego bruising is a common injury among musicians). They eventually left our group to form their own band.

It was about this time that I decided to leave the ancient corps that I had been a member of for the last six years. I was approaching fifty years old and it was getting to be a chore marching up and down those hills of New York and Connecticut while balancing a thirty pound pickle barrel drum on my leg. Many of the older members that I had become friends with were leaving, and the corps decided to admit female members to fill up the ranks. I have never doubted the ability of the fairer sex to toot a fife or beat a drum, but the corps gatherings would no longer have the same atmosphere. I had been there, done that, and didn't care to do it again. You know, water and oil and that sort of thing.

The next dance band was comprised of musicians that all had the unfortunate experience of going through a divorce. Naturally we named the group "The second time around" This band had a female vocalist. I always considered a female vocalist a plus for a band especially if she was good looking. (and she was) We developed a new list of songs to suit her voice and developed a pretty good sound again. I always believed in avoiding songs with tonal complexity in favor of doing the standard tunes well. She didn't mind giving up the mike when I would do a number so we didn't experience the ego thing with this band. Our new base player had a fondness for the "weed" but otherwise was a good musician. He graduated with a biology major and had a burning desire to become an Ibm'r. We had a great rhythm guitar player but he was relocating and we had to replace him. The replacement was always tuning up, It seemed the sound of his instrument never pleased him. One thing that irritated me with him was that he never could do the guitar lead—in on color my world. Because of that, I always thought the song was lacking when we performed it. Our vocalist had a mid life crisis one time and decided she was done with music. Our pleading with her fell on deaf ears and she left. We found a young girl that never sang with a band and she filled in for a couple of months. She had a dope smoking beau that followed her on every gig and got high as a kite every time. Thankfully, the crisis passed quickly and we welcomed our girl back with open arms. We played a wedding for a co worker who fancied himself a singer. It was one of the fancier venues in the area. Unbeknown to the band, most of the guests planned to leave the hall when he started singing, holding their noses. It didn't faze him a bit. We, the band members, were stunned.

I started taking piano lessons, sold my drums and purchased a piano. Then I started writing songs. I have them professionally recorded and submit them to music publishers. A song is simply a short story told in three and a half minutes. All a song needs is a beginning, an end and a hook to be a good song. I have had a lot of fun with music, met a lot of nice people and some that weren't so nice. I sometimes think I put too much emphasis on music and let other things slide, but it's all in the past. I really enjoyed myself and entertained a lot of people. Today, the music scene has changed. The small week-end bands have been replaced by dee jays. I guess the bands priced themselves out of the market. I think too, that people have become more mercenary and just don't perform for the enjoyment they get from making music and entertaining people. There is a lot of solo work and karaoke being done at most venues and I think that takes a lot of the personal aspects of music from any event. Garage bands had a distinct sound and that can't be captured by canned music. I would gladly do it again if I had the chance. So lets just take it from the top and let the music play!!

Richard (Digger) Vogt

25—DOGGIE IN THE WINDOW

September 14, 2013

LOVE FOR SALE!!! That sign should be prominently displayed in the windows of all pet shops. For when you purchase a dog from a pet shop, you buy love. When you adopt a homeless dog from a shelter, or save an unwanted dog from a lonely dangerous life on the street, you get love. A dog doesn't care how rich or poor you are. They don't care if you are a beauty or a beast. Your physical attributes don't mean a thing to a dog. They just want to be your friend. For all you give them, they give you unconditional love in return. They're seldom grumpy, and are always up for any situation that comes their way. Their wagging tail when you walk through the door at the end of a bad day at work will always bring a smile to your face. They just want to please you.

I have had a dog ever since I was a child. As I observed their behavior under conditions both good and bad, it is interesting to watch their reaction to a situation. It almost appears that they can sometimes read your mind. They anticipate your actions before they take place, and certainly do get to know your routine. If you lay your clothes on the bed and take a shower, they know that you are going somewhere. Bang your thumb with a hammer and let loose with a few nasty words, they head for the safest place of refuge. Open a can with the electric opener and they are right there with their tail wagging to beat the band. Give them a treat at a certain time every day, and they will let you know when the time has arrived with what seems like a built in alarm clock. My dogs have constantly amazed me with their insight.

Their instinctive behavior has always been a wonder to me. It is fascinating to watch them prepare their bed on the bare floor, scratching and fluffing up imaginary bedding so that they will be comfortable in their slumber. When offered a treat and they have a full belly, they will bury it under the corner of a throw rug and go through the motions of pushing dirt over it.

As soon as their eyes open after birth, they can swim, even though they never had a lesson. From the mixed breed to the pure bred, they all have that instinct in them dating back thousands of prior years when their ancestors roamed wild all over the globe.

A study was conducted at a university to determine if dogs had the power of extra sensory perception (esp). They placed video cameras in the home of a woman who had a dog to observe the dogs reaction to the woman's movements when away from home. They found that when the woman (who was visiting a friend miles away) announced to her host that she would be leaving to go home, the dog arose from sleeping on the floor and started pacing the room and wagging his tail. Inconclusive perhaps, but it does spur the imagination.

I have been a volunteer at animal shelters as long as I can remember. I have been a dog walker, dog transporter, kennel cleaner and have sponsored dogs at adoptathons. The two that live with us now were adopted from a shelter. They are Tibetan Spaniels and I always tell my wife that they hit pay dirt when they came to live with us. To me, dogs are just dogs.

But to my wife, they are little people and she treats them accordingly. Grooming, nails done, special foods and plush sleeping quarters. One has lost sight in one eye due to a growth on her eyeball, but it doesn't slow her down a bit. The other one underwent surgery twice due to a cancer on her leg and as a result has only three legs. Again, so what! She never lets on that it is gone.

I have had ten dogs in my life and how they came to live with me is unusual and sometimes eerie. One, a german shepard, I acquired through a girl who sang in a band that I had. She came to a rehearsal one night with this little ball of fur and asked if I would give it a home. It seems that her brother had a dog that had puppies and when they were weaned, he drove them to the local animal shelter and dropped them off. Unbeknown to him, one of the dogs had escaped from the box in the car. Gretchen now had a home and was with me for seventeen years. Another happened while I collected stones for a fireplace I was building in my home. The county was blasting the side of a stone mountain away on a major highway near my home. I drove over to the site with my truck to see if I could get some good stones for the job. When I pulled the truck off the highway, there was barely enough room to squeeze the vehicle alongside the stone piles. As I got out of the truck and started picking through the stones to get those best suited for a fireplace, heavy traffic was rushing past on one side with a sheer stone wall on the other. As I picked through the stones, a tiny puppy came walking out from a stone pile. How he got there, I'll never know. I didn't want to believe that anyone would be heartless enough to leave a small puppy along a heavily traveled highway. It seemed that he just dropped out of the sky. I picked him up, put him in the truck and another wayward dog had a home. Naturally, I named him Rocky. He was a great companion and the only dog that I ever saw that could smile. I don't mean just show his teeth, he actually smiled. (hold that pose! click!) Unfortunately, I never got a picture.

Rocky was a resident in our home for about three years and he was just a great dog. One day when I got home from work, Rocky was gone! I scoured the neighborhood for a week looking for him to no avail. I put an ad in the lost and found column of the local newspaper and got no response to it. I put posters up on telephone poles and nobody called. I even questioned a few locals who were known to keep their ear to the round, but had no luck finding Rocky. It was then I began to wonder. Maybe he did just fall out of the sky!

At one time, we had a German Shepard (Gretchen) a cat (Nicole) and a mini toy poodle (Suzette). With those three living in the house, we didn't need any other entertainment. The German Shepard and the cat tolerated each other pretty well. But the cat didn't have any use for the poodle. Of course, the poodle thought the cat would make a good playmate, but kitty didn't quite see it that way. To her, the poodle was just an interloper who upset the natural order of balance in the household. It was a bit of a job keeping the poodle and the cat separated, but with a few child gates on the doorways and a little vigilance, we managed to avoid the possibility of Suzette losing an eyeball to the cat.

When we travel, which is often, we usually take the dogs with us. The exception is when we are traveling overseas. There is a booklet distributed by the AAA organization that lists all the motels in the U S A that accept pets and list the conditions that apply when lodging with them. I rented a condo in Myrtle Beach one year on the recommendation of a friend who told me that dogs were welcome there. But when we got there, huge signs were posted that announced their policy on pets. NOT ALLOWED!! Fortunately our dog at the time was a mini poodle and she was easy to conceal going through the guarded entrance. The units were  sparsely occupied so we didn't have a problem. In fact, we were the only occupants in an eight unit building.

Dogs are playing a more important role in everyday life now with the emergence of therapy dogs and companion dogs. There are more dog parks available to pet owners and many restaurants will allow dogs to accompany their owners while they dine. I myself dont think dogs should be allowed to ride in shopping carts in the food stores, but that is quite common in some stores today. Of course, that is something that I'm sure will be settled by the health department in the near future. When I attend the various outdoor fairs that take place in my area, I see many people with their dogs on leashes at the event. This too, should be stopped. The dogs swelter in the heat and most people don't think to bring water for them, consequently the dogs suffer. They would rather be laying around home in air conditioned comfort, I'm sure.

I live in a subdivision where most of the residents have dogs. Unfortunately, many residents don't accept the responsibility that goes with being a dog owner. There are probably more arguments and feuds started between neighbors over dogs than any other cause. I have seen people that refuse to pick up after their dogs. When confronted, they act as though they are being unduly persecuted. I will never understand that kind of behavior from people.

Others will take a dog, tie it to an outdoor location and never have any contact with the animal except to feed it. They shouldn't be allowed to have dogs. Dogs are pack animals, they want to be with a group, have companionship. Isolation is the worse thing they can endure.

Today, dogs play a vital role in medicine and security. Dogs are used to sniff out cancers that might go undetected by medical testing equipment. They are also an asset in treating patients suffering from anxiety and other Physiological illness. They play a vital role in the treatment of nursing home patients who are feeling the pangs of loneliness, or in children s hospitals where the little ones can have contact with a bundle of love. They are essential in warfare, whether it be against an enemy that threatens our national security or in the constant war against drugs that imperil the future of the country. Dogs are one of our most valuable natural resources. What would we do without'em?

Richard (Digger) Vogt

26—HAPPY NEW YEAR

October 1, 2013

Me and my used to be wife received an invitation to a new years eve party to be held at a friends house which was about five miles from our home. After checking our social calendar and considering the possibility of foul weather, we decided we would attend the party and ring in the new year with a crowd of revelers we knew rather than stay home with Dick Clark or in some club with complete strangers. In previous years, anyone who stayed home was treated to the music of Guy Lombardo and his Royal Canadians. He had quite a large orchestra and was probably the best around. He played in a ballroom in New York City. The men wore tuxedos and the women always wore evening gowns, it was quite a classy affair. He was sometimes referred to as "Guy Lumbago" in a good natured way.

Going to a party meant dressing to the nines. Suit, Tie, and a nice semi formal dress for the ladies. Dungarees were strictly for yard work. When we left the house, we were dressed for a wedding reception. We looked "spiffy" When we got to the party we found a decent sized crowd who were whooping it up for the last time of the year. Some wore the traditional goofy party hats while others just lounged around trying to figure out the guests. Captain Jack was in attendance along with Samuel Adams and a few others known to fire up a crowd. As the night wore on the chosen few were getting ramped up for the road to stupidville. The crowd got louder and as the bubbly flowed, a couple of the guys looked as if they were ready for the lamp shade, and the wallflowers were starting to blossom. I have always wanted to take a video of the guests at the beginning of a party like this and take a second video of the same guests about four hours later. Many would become teetotalers after the second showing.

Well, we welcomed the new year in with a nice buffet and then the crowd just gathered in little groups for chit chat. Eventually, these chit chats get around to a serious discussion of politics and that is not a good thing considering the state of mind of most of the party goers. As the crowd started to thin out, I was in heated political debate with the host that was going nowhere. He being of one party affiliation and I another. Now the crowd really started to depart for calmer waters. Out of the clear blue sky, the host invites me outside to "Duke It Out" in his driveway. For those of you not familiar with street jargon that means "Mortal Combat". Not one to turn down a challenge, I gracefully accepted.

Here we are at two in the morning standing in the snow filled driveway, Dressed for a business meeting and slightly disheveled. He throws a haymaker at me, I throw one at him and we're rolling in the snow filled gravel. Now, my used to be comes out the door, takes one look, gets in the car and drives away in disgust. My host realizes the futility of the situation and goes back in the house, and I head toward his back yard to walk home. Big mistake!

Not being familiar with the neighborhood in which he lived, I figured if I kept walking, I would run across a road. I trudged on through the snow and finally came to a three strand barbed wire fence. I tried slipping through the two strands and felt the barbs grab the back of my jacket like a cats claws on a wool sweater. As I would back off the claws would release. Forward motion and they pulled. Then I felt the jacket rip all the way down the back. It was dark as a coal mine and I was straining to see in front of me. Suddenly a black face appeared, then another, and another face, and then another. All I could think was uh oh! What had I run into here? Black angus cattle was the answer, a herd of Black angus cattle. The only danger was maybe stepping in a meadow muffin.

I finally shouldered my way through the herd and came to a brook about twenty feet wide. I could see a thin layer of ice on the brook but I knew I had to get across it. (There's never a boat around when you need one). I took the first step and could feel the effect of the ice cold water go through my body. I maneuvered my way across the stream, slipping on the polished stones and breaking through the ice in spots until I reached the opposite side. I kept going and came upon a dirt road. In the distance, I could see a light so I headed in that direction and finally came upon an old farm house. I recognized the house as one belonging to the foreman on the cattle ranch that I had just come across. I figured hell, what have I got to lose? Im freezing, there is nothing else around, and I don't think I'll be able to walk home tonight. I walked up on the porch and rang the doorbell. (its about three o'clock in the morning). A man answered the door and appeared to be in shock when he saw me. "Where in gods name did you come from?" were the first words out of his mouth. I was wet up to my knees, disheveled, wearing a suit with the back of the jacket ripped open and unable to enunciate my words properly due to my frigid condition. He invited me in, gave me a blanket' pointed to the couch and told me to bunk there for the night. I settled in on the couch happy to be in out of the cold. (That kind of hospitality doesn't exist today).

When I awoke a few hours later, I was staring into the face of a blue uniformed man with a badge on his shirt. Startled is the only word I can use to describe how I felt at that moment. He told me that he was a guard at the local hotel for the bad guys (prison) and that he and a few other guards boarded at this home during the week. He invited me out to the kitchen where I dined on bacon and eggs with him and a half dozen other guards. I explained my situation to them and they had a grand old time predicting just what my future held in store for me when I got home. They were actually enjoying my situation, probably glad it wasn't happening to them. One told me he would rather go and face eighteen hundred inmates than to face the music that I was going to hear.

Well, my benefactors gave me a ride down to the general store which was located about two miles from my house where I had another cup of coffee. When I finally got up the courage to call my house, my used to be refused the call. I started up the road hoping I would get a ride from someone, anyone, but there is not much stirring on new years day so I had to make the hike on foot. And the worst wasn't over yet. Lesson learned!

Richard T Vogt

27—MY WEDDING

MAY 22 2012
Wedding Date May 1977

As weddings go, mine was a nice affair with fun loving guests and families of both me and my wife a bit standoffish. Each were eying the other with skepticism due to the minimal background both had on each other. The church service moved along and when we toasted our undying love to each other, it was done with grape juice rather than wine due to the restrictions the church had on imbibing alcohol within the hallowed halls of the holy enclosure. This was a second wedding for me and the first for my new wife. I was 44 years old and my wife had just turned 23 which produced a lot of doubt among the audience. Longevity for our merger wasn't foremost in most peoples minds. In fact I'm sure some were looking for a quick end to this madness. And then there were some who were hoping for it. Me, a musician, my wife a nurse, and we both had lifestyles to match our professions. I was the life of the party kind of guy with an opinion on just about any subject and my wife was quietly sedate with a live and let live type outlook on life. My three children reluctantly attended the wedding and wore a look that said they would rather be anywhere else than where they were. Following the church service, we motored to the reception hall where the band kept referring to my wife by my nickname "Mrs Digger", due to the fact that they didn't know my real name nor did they care. Now, this didn't go over too well with my wife's family who weren't into nicknames, musicians, wine toasts in church and generally anything that lacked seriousness at such an occasion. Well, we managed to tie the knot without any mishaps or having someone stand when the preacher said "if anyone has reason to believe these two should not be married, let them speak now" (I'm sure there were an abundance of reasons, but fortunately, no one had the courage or desire to stand and add two more enemies to their list. After the usual wedding ride through the streets with horns honking to the delight of the few gawkers along the way, we finally arrived at the location where our reception would be held. We planned the wedding at the V.F.W. hall not only because we were on a limited budget but because I found out over the years playing at many wedding receptions that it isn't the location of the reception that determines the success or failure of the event. It is the people who are in attendance. Invite a bunch of stuffed shirts and you will have a quiet, boring reception. I played in the band at a reception for a West Point cadet wedding and it was as dull as a Republican Club meeting. On the other hand, firehouse weddings with the right people in attendance really gives new meaning to the phrase "party time".

The reception was held in the afternoon and I had hired a four piece band. To further alienate my wife's family, when the band played the first song which was my cue to dance with my lovely wife and be introduced for the first time as husband and wife, they did it with a flourish but introduced us as Mr. and Mrs. Digger. Bong!!!! The reception was a lively affair due to an open bar and an insatiable thirst on the part of most of the invited guests. I kept the band and open bar going for an extra hour much to the delight of those attendees that were slightly awash in the bubbly. When the festivities came to an end and my wife had changed to her honeymoon dress, we picked up our bags and went out to get into our chariot for the ride to our hotel in the Big Apple.

The limo which was hired by my wife based on a friends recommendation was quite a surprise. I expected to see a sleek, long, shiny black Cadillac or Lincoln sitting out in front waiting to whisk us to the airport, but instead we were greeted by two matronly women sitting in a ten year old Dodge four door sedan. So much for the recommendation of friends. Well, off we go into the wild blue highway and head for New York City where we will spend the night in a honeymoon suite before flying down to Bermuda. The ride down to the city was certainly one to remember. As we started down the darkened parkway to The Big Apple, the headlights of the car went out for no apparent reason. This prompted a shriek from our matronly chauffeur followed by her assurance that they would "come right back on" which they did. This occurred every few miles followed by her shriek and assurances that it was only temporary. I told my wife to sit back and close her eyes.

As we neared the city of Yonkers, the driver turned and asked if we minded her stopping in the city so that she could drop off her mother and some of her packages to which we agreed. After unloading what seemed like a busload of packages from the trunk, we were on our way again. New York City traffic is heavy and as we sped down a heavily traveled road, I spotted a dog coming down an embankment and heading for the road. All of a sudden the car lights went out, I felt a bump, heard a shriek, and bowser was on his way to the doggie spirit world. Thankfully, we arrived at our hotel a short time later. We opted for a bridal suite in the hotel which was to come with a few amenities such as a bottle of champagne which when I inquired about it, the bell hop described it by holding up a thumb and forefinger to indicate it was only an" itty bitty thing". So much for champagne. I decided to get some ice for our drinks and left the room dressed only in slacks. No shirt, no shoes or socks. I had to go to the next floor to get the ice and I remembered that I not only forgot the key to our room, but I forgot the room number. Down to the lobby I go half dressed and carrying an ice bucket. (no one even gave me a glance). Ahhh! Good old liberal New York City. I sheepishly went over to the main desk and asked not only for a key to my room, but also just what room I was in. After calling my wife and getting verification that this half dressed man was her husband. The desk clerk laughingly gave me a key.

The honeymoon in Bermuda flew right by and we were on our way home in a van driven by the husband of the woman who drove us down. As soon as he punched the gas pedal, I knew both he and his frau were graduates of the same driving school. (I would guess Joey Chitwood's). We happened to be passing Yankee stadium as a baseball game ended and the crowd was leaving. He was changing lanes at fifty miles an hour with no regard for signals or other cars and when he found a clear stretch of road, the van would lurch forward like a rocket. There was another couple in the van with us but not a word was spoken all the way home. Terror will do that! We made it home in one piece and when I got out of the van, I kissed the driver instead of my brand new wife. Anxiety will sometimes produce that kind of erratic behavior. Seriously, check out your ride before hand, make sure it is what you are expecting.

I'm happy to say that, despite our age difference and a variety of other contradictions in our lives, we are still happily married after thirty six years of marraige.

Richard (Digger) Vogt

28—HEART ATTACK TIME

DECEMBER 15, 2013

It was just another Monday morning, another work week. I was sitting at my desk after the usual cafeteria breakfast of greasy sausage and egg on a hard roll when I felt a sharp pain in my chest. I thought it was just a little indigestion, but after an hour I started to question my own judgment. When the discomfort continued and I got alarmed, I asked a co-worker who happened to be walking down the hall if he would escort me to the first aid area. As soon as I got there they ran a battery of simple tests and deduced that I had all the symptoms of a heart attack.

They contacted my immediate manager who came down and told me that a co-worker in our department would be taking me to the hospital which was about fifteen miles away. Now you have to see this co-worker to realize that this was the worst decision possible. He weighed about three hundred fifty pounds and had the disposition of a mule. I walked out, got in his station wagon and away we go. The poor guy was more nervous than I was, and at every red light when I urged him to go through, he simply told me that he wasn't going to risk a ticket. I kept thinking to myself "what in the hell are they doing? Imagine the liability on the company if the grim reaper came for me during that ride? Lucky for me, we didn't have to stop for gas or change a flat.

I should clear something up here. My personal life was in a quandary before this happened. I had gone through a divorce, was playing in a band and keeping late hours, and to top it all off I married a girl twenty one years younger than I was all within a year. All that might present a challenge to the ticker. But I was only forty four years old and felt that I was twenty four.

My heart was still beating when we got to the hospital so that part went well. They wheeled me in and put enough wires on me to make it appear I had a date with "Old Sparky" down in Sing Sing Prison. I was in the hospital for eighteen days and think that I had every test that was available. The pains persisted despite all the medical assistance available to me. I had stress tests followed by a radioactive scan of the heart under a huge circular disc that pressed up against my face as I lay flat on a table. That really put my claustrophobia to the test. I left the hospital with severe pains in my chest.

I subsequently had an angiogram performed which showed a slight blocking of the arteries and I was put on medication. The doctor treating me at the time was puzzled. I would go out and walk nine holes of golf with a chest pain that would send most men to the E.R. The doctor had me keep a daily diary so that I would record when the pains started, stopped, and the severity of them, every day for a month. Nothing ! I was an enigma. It was decided that I should undergo another angiogram. I didn't want to have it through the groin because that method required the patient to lay flat on their back without moving for eight hours. I wanted to have the procedure performed through my arm which meant I could stand almost immediately afterward. They found a doctor in Albany who was skilled in that method and away we go! Again, not enough blockage to justify the pain I was experiencing. Because I got released from the hospital at night, we got lost in the city of Albany. Now, that is a scary experience for two country bumpkins from Poughquag. I should note here that a few years later we lived in Albany for three months and I got to know the city like the back of my hand and I actually enjoyed the place.

When I had my heart attack, I was living a rough life style. I was smoking, drinking, and following a diet that was fit for only a Viking. I saw the light and decided to clean up my act. I gave up all my vices and to this day, I haven't had a drop of alcohol, smoked a cigarette, or eaten a piece of red meat. That was forty years ago. While on vacation at the beach in Maryland, I noticed a paperback book on the shelf by a doctor claiming to know the secret to reversing heart disease. It was just a vegetarian diet which had to be strictly adhered to. I decided to try it out for a while and my wife joined me. We were eating only vegetables along with an occasional dish of pasta. Soon, my palate was yearning for more variety. We tried eating tofu as a substitute for meat, but it just didn't satisfy either our hunger or our taste buds. (It was really pretty bad). I sent away for an order of twenty prepared meals that were specific for a vegetarian diet. They arrived packed in dry ice and we started devouring them. The first few meals were a novelty and we pretended to enjoy them, but as we worked our way into the freezer, we had to admit that eating these tasteless meals was like eating the newspaper the fish came wrapped in. We finally tossed them into the garbage and went back to our heart disease reversing diet of just veggies and pasta which we had grown to tolerate pretty well.

My wife became concerned that we weren't getting sufficient protein following the diet that we chose so she made an appointment with a nutritionist. After explaining our diet to her, and our reason for the drastic change in our eating habits, the nutritionist agreed that our diet was not providing a sufficient amount of protein and suggested that we include a portion of red meat into our meals at least three times a week. I balked at this suggestion but did compromise to a point where I would occasionally eat fish or fowl. I am an animal activist and I realized that eating red meat did not not coincide with my beliefs. I have been following this meat free diet for forty years and although it complicates my social life a bit, I find it very manageable and we have no trouble planning meals. I am always amused by people that we meet who say, after we reveal that we don't eat red meat. "Oh! we only eat red meat about once or twice a week". We have had times when we get invited out to dinner where the hostess will serve red meat despite our avoiding it and we don't indulge, we just eat the sides. I never could figure out whether it was our commitment or not breaking it that seemed to annoy some of our host's. Sure I miss a good old greasy hamburger or a breaded veal cutlet once in a while. I salivate when we pass a steakhouse and the inviting odor of a nice filet mignon comes wafting through the night air, but I don't veer off my diet. I am convinced that avoiding red meat has aided me in reversing my heart problem.

My wife and I decided to move to Florida, and when we did, we started all over again. Everything was new to us. It's a new life, everything changes. I've known people who live down here who keep their doctors up north when they make their move to the southland. Not me, I immediately found a new cardiologist who started a new approach to my heart problem. After a thorough exam, I had a angiogram where it was discovered that new capilliary vessels were forming around the blocked arteries of my heart. But this doctor was also puzzled that I was experiencing such persistent pains in my chest. He suggested that maybe my pains were arthritic and placed me on an anti inflammatory drug. I credit that, and something I discovered on my own with eliminating the chest pains I suffered with for twenty years. I found that when I slept on my left side for a couple of days, the familiar chest pain would reoccur. I still don't think my cardiologist believes it, but it is true! But a healthy lifestyle is of paramount importance. People are like snowflakes, no two are exactly the same. A solution to one persons ailments may act negatively on another person. To this day, if I sleep on my left side for a few days, I get the same chest pains that I experienced fifteen years ago. There are many factors to consider when addressing heart trouble, but a healthy life style is of paramount impotence.

I walk two miles every day, not just some days but every day. I walk eighteen holes of golf a week even though my scores don't back that up. I have had plenty of friends who abused their body and they went to an early grave. I have seen young guys brag about their pot belly's, bragging how much they spent on beer to grow that unsightly pouch. But they will pay the price as they get older. Yes, I know some friends of mine who have abused their bodies and enjoyed the high-life that are still going strong. That is the exception rather than the rule. The body is like some what like an automobile but you can't trade it in for a new model.

Richard T Vogt

29—THE NEW GARAGE

December 14, 2013

I was getting tired of seeing my cars full of dust and grime stirred up by the traffic going by our house and decided I would build a two car garage to replace the original garage which I had remodeled into a beautiful recreation room. I dont mean actually build it myself but to contract out the various construction steps need to complete it. The first step was to obtain a building permit. I lived in a small town at the time where just about everything was done on a handshake and sometimes there would be a transfer of money between those hands to finalize the agreement. The fee for the building permit was usually an amount determined by what kind of mood the inspector was in that particular day. I recall he was wearing his smiley face the day I approached him and I didn't have to dig too deep. This interaction occurred prior to the town adopting new zoning laws and building codes to accommodate the frantic building of homes which allowed half of New York City to move up to the country. The diary farms were gone and in their place were the refugees from the Big Apple seeking a safe environment in an area that they could reconstruct to their standards.

The first thing I had to do was to dig a trench for the foundation. I hired someone who owned a septic tank business to dig the trench and also dig up some drain pipe that I wanted to replace. When he arrived, I had second thoughts about his competency. The truck looked like it it was out of the Mad Max movie set, and the backhoe bucket had a tooth missing from it. Come to think of it, when the backhoe operator smiled, he resembled the bucket. When he commenced digging the trench alongside my house, he called me over and pointed out the fireplace chimney attached to the side of the house. "No foundation under it" he said, "It will collapse if I keep digging". I grabbed a shovel and kept scraping away the dirt until I discovered the foundation. Now that he was sure the fireplace chimney wasn't going to topple over on his back hoe, the operator commenced digging the trench so that a footing could be poured.

The next step was the foundation which would be constructed using cement blocks. I contacted a mason and negotiated a price for laying the block and sat back and waited, and waited, and waited. The mason never showed up. When I called his home to find out why he was delayed, his wife informed me that he had passed away, and suggested I contact his brother in law who was also a mason. I am a spiritual person and I thought that maybe it would portend a dire outcome if I called him so I declined. I decided to lay the block myself, even Though I had never laid a block. I was young and adventurous and thought "nothing ventured nothing gained". Once the footings were poured, I squared it up, staked it, and I was now a working mason. I got the surprise of my life after about an hour of handling the concrete blocks. I looked at the palms of my hands and they looked like I pressed them against a belt sander, they were raw. Lesson learned, use canvas gloves.

The next step required a carpenter and I was fortunate (I thought) to locate one quickly in the local job column in the newspaper. When the guy reported the first day, he reeked of alcohol and his eyes looked like he had been up all night. I nipped that in the bud (no pun intended) by asking him if he was licensed and if he had liability insurance. He didn't, and I embarked on a new carpenter search. The next guy was sober, insured, and didn't seem to have any baggage so he was my man. The framing progressed well for a few days and then it happened, my man didn't show up Monday and again Tuesday. I then found out that like a lot of us, he had women problems on top of his cash flow problems. (you cant have one without the other). Despite his problems, he managed to complete the framing in a reasonable time and told me he was moving out of the state. The third carpenter was a lulu. He never stopped talking, but fortunately his hands kept moving. He was full of suggestions on how to not only customize my garage but also how to customize my life. He claimed to be a man of the world, but rather than give off an air of the Greek poet Homer, he had the demeanor of the Army private Gomer. But none the less, he was a good, steady worker. He closed up the structure in no time and after I paid him for his labor, he told me he was going to resume his college career and get a degree in political science. I just knew he would do well because he had a natural ability to twist a story.

I hired a redi-mix cement truck to pour the floor and when the driver arrived, he was surprised that it would need so much cement (he called it mud). When he started pouring the mud from the chute, me and my buddy could hardly keep up. I had made a wood float to spread the cement around and level it after it was poured. Not being familiar with the tool. I made it about fourteen inches wide. When the driver saw it, he jumped out of the truck and exclaimed "what are you gonna to do with that toy"? When he got done laughing, he proceeded to make one himself in no time which was about three feet wide and would move a lot of the ceement (southern pronunciation). Cement has to be worked quickly for as soon as it is exposed to air it starts to set up (harden) and stays that way forever.

Then the driveway had to be paved. The blacktop company cut all the lawn out in sections of sod so I could move it up to the graveled area I had been using for a driveway in front of the old garage. My wife and I laid all that sod down dirt side up and then raked it and planted grass seed. The next spring it had grown into a beautiful lawn. I thought one of the steps they used in the blacktopping process was a bit unusual. When they had spread the hot blacktop on the full surface of the driveway area, they first raked it smooth and then had one of the young guys strap sections of flat wooden board to his feet. Then, using tiny sideways steps he tamped down the entire area while the hot blacktop was cooling. This serves to exemplify the need for a good education. All students should strive for excellence in school, otherwise they could someday be doing a Fred Astaire routine with boards strapped to their feet, tamping down hot black top in anywhere U.S.A.

I spent those cold winter nights down in the cellar building a cupola for the roof. It would not only look quaint on the roof, but would also provide ventilation on those hot summer days. I had a few people stop and ask where I purchased it and when I told them I built it, they wanted me to build another for them. I explained that I was a novice at carpentry and if I did build one for them and charged for my labor, it would probably cost ten thousand dollars. That usually got a double take and a quick goodbye from them. When I finally sold my house years later, I had to make quite a few structural upgrades due to the lack of building codes when I built the garage. I did additional remodeling to the house over the years and always hired a contractor who was qualified to do the complete renovation rather subcontract the job out. It is important to research the work history of anyone you hire, the wrong contractor can end up giving you nightmares. Lesson learned, look before you leap!

Richard T Vogt

30—PIANO LESSONS

December 12, 2013

I played in bands as a drummer for most of my life and although I enjoyed my instrument, I always envied the people who were what I considered the musical part of the band. They were able to read those dots and lines on the paper in front of them when we were playing a tune. Those dots and lines were sheet music. It was a puzzle to me. When they would call a tune in the key of "G" or "F" I always knew what it meant but really didn't understand it. I vowed that I would someday learn to read music. It is universal, it knows no language barrier and is the common denominator when joining other musicians for what is known as a "jam session". If you have music. no rehearsal is needed, just take it from the top and let the good times roll.

When I retired from the company that I worked for after thirty four years, I was given a supplemental payment of twenty five hundred dollars to use as I saw fit to enable me to transition into retired life. Some went back to school in order to further their education. Some took courses which would enable them to move into the field of service work. I knew one fellow who bought a new set of golf clubs (which were disguised as golf lessons), some new golf clothing. and spent the rest on green fees. I figured that now was a good time to learn to play the piano. I had a piano in my home that we purchased for my wife who took lessons previously and could play rather well. I figured I had enough experience playing with bands that I could learn on my own. I quickly realized where the Confucian saying "he who teaches himself has a fool for a pupil" originated. Unless a person is gifted, it is impossible to do.

I located a class in one of the local malls sponsored by Yamaha and given to group classes for a moderate fee. I guess they figured that you would buy one of their instruments after you bought your tour bus. I was having my own piano tuned and discussed my plan with the man doing the tuning who told me that while group lessons were good for the basics, I would advance more quickly with a private instructor. I searched the local newspaper and found a young girl who recently graduated from Oberlin College with a degree in music and had a music studio where she taught piano. I called her and arranged my initial lesson. I really felt foolish when I sat down at the piano for the first time. Here is a girl about twenty one years old and I am fifty nine. It seemed that the teacher was being taught by the student. I had to overcome that feeling of awkwardness in order to benefit from the instruction I was being given. I never questioned her credentials, She was more than qualified having graduated from on of the best music schools in the country. She had a gift for teaching and was open minded to my needs.

When I started taking lessons, I had a discussion with my instructor about how deep I wanted go into learning the piano. I explained that foremost in my intention was to be able to read and write music. Then I wanted to learn the basics of the keyboard so that I could entertain myself with pop tunes and standards. I didn't want to get into theory or become a classical pianist. With that goal agreed upon between us, I progressed well. It is a lot of hard work learning any instrument, but the the rewards are beyond description. It requires hour upon hour of repetitious practice and a bit of indulgence from anyone within earshot. It requires a lot of patience and determination which is sometimes difficult to maintain when you sit down to practice and nothing seems to fit together, and believe me, there are days like that. Too many people start off with good intentions but get bored because they don't see rapid improvement. It is a slow gradual process and requires perseverance. Eighty percent of the people who purchase pianos with the intention of learning the instrument never do. Now that is a sad statistic.

I remember a humorous incident that happened one day that is worth mentioning. My teacher had a rather large Labrador retriever who was very protective of his turf. Well, one day I arrived early and entered the downstairs studio before the teacher arrived from her home upstairs. I heard a loud rustling on the stairs and was suddenly confronted by a very annoyed dog with fangs bared. My attempt to calm him not only went unheeded, it made him more aggressive. I kept calling her and finally she arrived, and I think saved me from certain mutilation which would have ended my musical career before it got off the ground. She did finally have to get rid of the dog because of his aggressive nature. A recital was scheduled for her students where she could show the parents where their hard earned money was going and she asked me to do a number. I was hesitant at first, but with a little reassurance from her, I reluctantly agreed to perform the song "Stardust" by Hoagy Carmicheal (by the way, Hoagy had help on the song by a man named Mitchell Parish Who never really gets any credit for it.) When the crowd arrived for the recital, the parents were eying me with suspicion and asking my teacher why I was there. When the time came for my number, I was as nervous as a squirrel in an eagles nest. But I managed to perform the tune to the satisfaction of the entire audience and the delight of my teacher.

I studied with her for about three years and achieved my goal under her expert guidance. I could read and write music, and play just about anything that was written. Now I was in a position to pursue another of my ambitions, song writing. I went on to write about fifty songs which I am trying to find a market for as of this writing. The song writing industry is a difficult field to enter. The business now is controlled by large conglomerates and unless lady luck is lurking in the background, success for a novice songwriter is virtually non-existent. Many songwriter credits are given because of the influence someone might have in the music world or because of a person's notoriety. Paul Anka wrote the theme song for the Johnny Carson show and gave Johnny co-writer credit for the tune. Whether Johnny was involved in the writing of the song is anybody's guess. I read that they earned six point two million dollars for that song. Just think about it, His show ran for twenty five years and the tune was the intro for the show every time it ran. Paul was quoted as saying it put his daughter through college.

I purchased a digital piano which has a built in rhythm section (Bass and drums) which produces a full sound when a song is played. There are many other features on it and it never has to be tuned. Learning the piano has been one of the highlights of my life. I manage to sit down and tickle the ivorys just about every day and never get tired of it. It is hard to describe the amount of pleasure I get from being able to sit down, hit some keys and make beautiful music. Maybe it is because I was a drummer and didn't create melody that I get so much enjoyment from it. I talk to so many people who envy musicians and aspire to learn an instrument, and my advice is always the same. Do it! The rewards are plentiful and there will never be any regrets.

Richard T Vogt

31—TRAVEL NURSING

September 3, 2013

My wife retired from a veterans hospital where she was employed as a registered nurse for twenty five years. She enjoyed working in her profession, so rather than become a non productive member of society, she chose to become a travel nurse. This job sector is what the name implies, they are nurses who fill positions in medical facilities where ever they are needed.

The first step is to sign on with a private company whose sole purpose is to contract with hospitals to provide them with nurses on a part time basis to fill in where their job skills are in demand. The company lists the names of facilities seeking help and the nurse/employee picks that facility which is located in an area which satisfies their needs. In most cases, the decision is strictly geographic. Such as someplace they have always wanted to visit, or it could be as simple as wanting to be in a warm climate during the winter.|

The pay scale is usually above what regular hospital nurses are paid and the benefits are many.

Every employee is provided with housing for their entire contract period and given financial travel compensation to their assignment location. They fully furnish any housing provided and allow a mate to live with the employee. There is a substantial bonus at the end of the contract period. An assignment could last from three months to a year. It is difficult work due to a number of reasons. There are different meds systems in every hospital, it takes time to get into the new routine when entering an unfamiliar work environment, and familiarization with the new co workers always requires tact and diplomacy.

The housing provided for my wife varied from apartments to elaborate condominiums and even a private home on the gulf of Mexico. On one assignment in Connecticut, we expected a guest for a couple of weekends and requested a two bedroom apartment. They did provide the apartment, but neglected to furnish the second bedroom. When notified, they had it furnished the next day. Not only did they comply quickly, they sent us a One hundred dollar dinner check.

The house on the gulf of Mexico had one of the best stocked librarys that I have ever seen, and all of the apartments provided pool service with exercise rooms. We stayed on the tenth floor of a high rise in Connecticut that provided twenty four hour concierge services. It was in July and we watched the fireworks in new New York City from the fooftop. There was one assignment where the apartment rules allowed only one dog. They did allow a dog and a cat, but only one dog. At the time we traveled with two dogs so we had to lease an apartment on our own at the last minute. We would be reimbursed for the cost. It was an apartment that we will long remember!!

About a week before we left Florida for an assignment in New York, we received the guidelines containing the rules for the apartment that was leased for us by the travel company. Much to our chagrin, we found out that our having two dogs violated the board of directors ruling on harboring pets in any apartment. We thought of just driving up and disregarding the rule, but being out on the street in a strange town wasn't very appealing to either of us. We searched the real estate section of the newspaper for available apartments in that area and found one in a house. By the time we got the contract in the mail, I had someone that I knew living in the vicinity do an appraisal of the neighborhood, and it wasn't good. I tore up the contract and started looking on the internet. I found an apartment in a small town near the hospital where my wife would be working and contacted the owner. (time was growing short). After the routine questions were passed back and forth between myself and the owner, I leased the apartment sight unseen.

A few days later, we embarked on what we always considered another adventure. After a two day drive we arrived at the site of the apartment. I was greeted not by the owner, but by a carpenter who was renovating a downstairs apartment for the owner. When I walked up the stairs to the apartment, I was shocked. The place was filthy. There were McDonald's cups and burger wrappings all over the floor. The stove looked like it hadn't been cleaned in years. The living room rug was so soiled that I didn't even want my dogs to walk on it. There were holes in the luan doors. The venetian blinds were covered with an oily grime, and the radiator cover in the lavatory was covered with rust.

I quickly called the owner and complained about the condition of the apartment. She arrived in about an hour. When she knocked, I opened the door and there stood a woman who looked like she didn't miss too many dinner bells. When I stated my case, she became very indignant and tried to put me on the defensive by stating that she violated her own rules regarding animals and gave us a break although we had two dogs. I do believe that she didn't think the place was as bad as I made it out to be. (through the eyes of the beholder)! We never really hit it off after that encounter. Well, my wife had to report to her new assignment in two days, not enough time to find another place to stay, so we unpacked and vowed to make the best of a bad situation.

We immediately got to work cleaning the place up. It took me about two hours to clean the stove surface at which time I discovered that it had only one functional burner. We soaked the blinds in the bathtub and they were much improved. The holes in the doors I concealed by hanging pictures over them. And then, there was the rug. I called the stanley steamer rug cleaners and they cleaned it the next morning. (although still full of stains, it was superficially clean). We probably removed a garbage can full of loose debris from the apartment. I sanded the rust off the radiator cover in the bathroom and painted it. I subsequently took the rug cleaning bill to the landlord for payment (100.00). She admonished me for having done it on my own and told me she had a woman who offered to clean it for fifty dollars.

During our three month stay, I guess I caught well over a dozen mice in traps there. We had one incident occur with a mouse that was funny. (The incident, not the mouse). I had placed a bucket under the sink because the drain would leak when the sink was emptied of water after washing the dishes. We were having supper one night and kept hearing a squeaking sound. I thought that maybe one of the children next door was riding a tricycle with a rusty wheel and disregarded it. It continued all through supper. I wondered about the strange behavior from our dogs who were running back and forth while yipping loudly. After cleaning up and washing the dishes, I drained the sink. When I emptied the bucket, there was a dead mouse in the water. We didn't hear the squeaking anymore!

The house was located on a main thoroughfare and we were serenaded by the hum of car tires all through the night. Whenever there was a thunderstorm, the power would fail, which in turn always tripped the breaker for the air conditioner. I would have to go to the apartment below, ask permission to enter, and reset the breaker. I'm sure this was a violation of even the weakest of electrical building codes, but the small town good old boy system works in strange ways. During our entire stay, there was some sort of noise most of the day from the carpenter remodeling the apartment downstairs. There was always some sort of construction in progress. Pounding, sawing, drilling. That was our music for the day. After we were living there for about two months, the landlady had a new stove installed. (with four working burners). We were preparing for supper one evening and one of the renovation workers came to the door and asked if he could paint the bathroom. Now, this really irritated me. We were living there for about two and a half months with the dingy paint on the bathroom walls and now they wanted to paint it for the new tenant, on my time. This led to a heated discussion between the landlady and me. When we left two weeks later, the bathroom was still not painted.

Needless to say, this travel experience was not typical. All of the previous excursions into the travel nurse world were pleasant and we still have fond memories of the different places we have stayed. It was always interesting visiting the different towns and citys and added a new dimension to my wife's resume.

Richard (Digger) Vogt

133

32—CHANGING PLACES

Jully 6, 2013

I was 68 years old and had lived in only two places in my entire life. Somehow it didn't seem right. My grandchild was six years old and had moved in and out of four homes. My wife was a registered nurse and was working for a company that arranged part time assignments for those in the medical profession, and after some discussion she accepted an assignment that would take us to the sunny state of Florida for three months. We buttoned up our house for the onslaught of winter, packed our bags and left upstate New York for our new adventure. It was in December, was very cold, and we were looking forward to those swaying palms and sunny days on the beach. It was raining and freezing on the road the day we left and as we traveled south, I was monitoring the temperature from the cockpit of my Buick, watching it rise as we slowly motored toward the state that many good naturedly refer to as "gods waiting room".

When we arrived in Florida, we were overwhelmed by the climate change. Just as the travel brochures claim, it was a paradise. No cold weather, ice on the windshield, or heavy clothes. We had found our Shangri-la. The housing boom hit hard in Florida and there were model homes of all styles and prices to look at. It didn't take long to adjust to this lifestyle. Picking a grapefruit off the tree in the backyard for breakfast, picking oranges for fresh juice, wearing summer clothes in January has its appeal. We started thinking about selling out in New York and moving south. One of the first places we looked at had six models to choose from and provided entertainment and food while we examined their dwellings. We subsequently looked at a dozen different models by different builders with all kinds of purchasing plans and just couldn't decide what to do. It was a big decision, and we weren't ready to make such a move. The three month assignment my wife accepted was about to terminate and we knew it was now or never. Driving home to our rental one day, we passed a billboard advertising the first models we had viewed and decided to have a second look at them. We went back, talked to an agent, looked at a lot, and signed on the dotted line. The die was cast, no turning back now. We would soon be living in the land of gators, geckos and early bird specials.

Our new home would be completed by the builder in November. That, coupled with the fact that my wife had accepted another assignment at a hospital in Connecticut meant we would have to adhere to an accelerated plan in order to dispose of our house in New York. I had resided in the house for forty years which meant I accumulated a lot of junk. Of course, I had to get rid of the junk. No easy task. I had the house appraised by a realtor and then contacted the county to obtain approval to sell it. (A dwelling must meet current building codes before it can be sold,) The inspection uncovered a few non conforming conditions as a result of remodeling over the forty year span that I lived there. (It was actually twice the size of the original house.) That done, we posted a for sale sign on the fence in front of the house and just sat and waited for the horde of buyers to beat a path to our door.

We had the usual curious neighbors just wanting to see how we lived, a couple who were living in a trailer, had no credit and wanted us to hold the mortgage and a few other assorted tire kickers. In the meantime, we were having garage sales, house sales, anything to get rid of our "stuff". At one of our sales, a young couple from new york city asked for a tour of the house and immediately offered to buy it at the asking price. They said they looked a dozens of homes and ours was the cleanest they had seen. Now we would have to be out of the house in two months which meant we had to find a place to live until my wife completed her assignment in Connecticut.

Finding a rental for three months isn't easy. We went to one motel that advertised short term leases and it was a disaster. An oriental woman was showing us the unit and kept slapping her palm against the wall. She said mosquitoes, but really roaches. The mice above the ceiling sounded like they were running rodent races. Nuf said? Bye bye!! We looked at a house in Connecticut that was deep in the woods and occupied by a family of four. It had an apartment on the second floor with a narrow, steep staircase that would be a daunting experience with an armload of groceries. The electric stove had wires protruding from all angles like an electronic octopus. This place was also a no no. My wife got a tip from one of the nurses that she worked with that the in laws of Micheal J Fox, the actor, had a guest house on their property that was unoccupied. My wife knocked on their door to inquire about renting it, but was told that Micheal and his family were moving into it shortly. (Really ??)

I hired contractors to bring the house up to the current building code standards and the buyer hired his own home inspector to examine the premises and uncover any possible flaws that would threaten his investment. (septic, well, radon gas, etc.) When the inspector arrived, I couldn't believe my eyes. He was my office mate at the manufacturing plant we both recently retired from. (talk about irony!) But he was a "by the book" type guy and I didn't expect him to look the other way if he found anything wrong. (the house passed-phew!!)

Closing day for the sale of the house arrived and we were still looking for a place to live. We finally put our furniture in storage and moved into a motel in the area. We would live in the cramped unit for six weeks. It was really a challenge. In order to watch the TV in the evening, I fashioned a sort of barrier around the tv with a large piece of cardboard that I salvaged from a local store and just kept the volume so low that I had to just about press my ear to the set to hear it. I did this so that my wife could get the sleep she needed for her twelve hour work day. She would arise very early and prepare for work. Her breakfast would be toast and coffee which she made in the bathroom so she in turn wouldn't wake me. (or wake our mini poodle-Suzette.)

I was going to sell my vehicle which was five years old and like new. I advertised it in the local newspaper and got an offer the next day. The potential customer gave me a five hundred dollar deposit and said he wanted to let his daughter look the SUV over before committing to buy it. He returned the next day with his daughter who was about ten years old and certainly wasn't old enough to drive. He requested a test drive and off we went. He drove like a maniac and much to my chagrin, told me he was a house painter and would use the vehicle in his business. I immediately envisioned my well maintained like new vehicle splattered with paint and full of dents. My fears were put to rest a few days later when he told me he couldn't get a loan because of bad credit as a result of going bankrupt recently. I told him I was withdrawing from the agreement and tore up the check. I had the SUV transported to Florida and still drive it daily as I have for twenty years.

We happily left the motel when my wife completed her assignment in Connecticut and drove to Florida where we found that our new home wouldn't be complete until February. Again, we needed a place to stay. My wife had an new assignment at a local hospital in a week, so we arranged for her employer to rent housing for the three months of her contract. Because of the residential building boom underway, there was a scarcity of workers which meant the build of our house was progressing at a snails pace. The poured concrete slab sat silent for weeks. We would joke about driving up to see our "slab". But then, they broke the backlog and the house became more real as each board or window was added and the landscapers moved in to create a garden like atmosphere on the property. We have been living in the house for twelve years now and are perfectly content. We made the right choice. Do I miss New York? Sure, I miss the mountains, the beautiful Hudson river, the shine of the moon reflecting off the frozen snow after a daytime thaw and the smell of wood burning in the fireplace. But the bone chilling cold and exorbitant taxes which meant digging down into the bank account were enough to justify the move.

Richard T. (Digger) Vogt

33—COOL MAN COOL

October 10, 2013

Living in Florida for most retirees means a life free of everyday drudgery. Enjoying life in the tropics the way it was meant to be. Whenever physical labor is required, it is usually performed by someone other than that person who will reap pleasure from that labor. There are salesman, glib of tongue, who could probably sell you the Brooklyn Bridge. There is a veritable army of craftsman ready to turn your humble abode into the Taj Mahal. (for a price) They will improve your life by installing new air conditioners, kitchen appliances, marble counter tops, clean the tile, replace the tile. Anything to make the little ladies happy.

All you have to do is ring them and like magic, they are at your door. Now the problem is that some of these people are honest and above board and do excellent work and some are not. Its the age old question," who are the good guys and who are the bad guys!!!" This article will highlight the pitfalls I encountered when buying a new air conditioner a few years ago.

My air conditioner was about ten years old and really showing signs of wear, so after a brief discussion, my wife and I decided to buy a new one. Age was not the only factor, The "SEER" ratings had changed quite a bit over the ten year span that we had ours and we would be buying a much more energy efficient unit. The unit we had was installed by the builder of the house and as is the case in subdivision homes, it was considered by many to a builders model. We decided to interview agents from two different air conditioning companies and decide after meeting with the representatives just which unit we would purchase. The first meeting was with a young fellow, selling a known brand who would also be installing the unit. As was to be expected, it had all the features most units have and came with a five year warranty and a good efficiency rating. The second agent also showed us a unit with a good efficiency rating, but offered a ten year warranty on all parts. It was a more expensive unit, but after negotiating a reduction in price, we closed a deal on the second offer.

Our new unit was installed on March 12, 2010. The installers seemed to be quite expert at what they did and in fact, one of them remarked to me that all he ever wanted to do was install air conditioning units. They seemed to know exactly what they were doing and in about two days, the installation was complete. The weather was still on the cool side so we really didn't need to start the unit right away although the technicians did start the unit and got it to produce ice cold air. Man, we felt like we were set for the next ten years. After all, it was brand new and guaranteed against all defects for that period. Bring on that hot sweltering humid Florida weather, we were ready!

Three days later, (apr 3rd)I noticed a pool of water on the floor under the air handler in the garage. I called the a/c company and a technician examined it. His determination was that the unit was not properly installed and should not be used until the proper corrections were made. He was supposed to return the next day (apr 4th). The next day, I waited until three in the afternoon and called the company. The receptionist told me that they did not have an available technician to come to my house and that I should just turn the unit back on and disregard the leak. The next day (Apr 5th) a technician came and fixed the leak. Subsequently, it was series of breakdowns. It got to the point that I was supplied with a portable a/c unit to be placed in my bedroom because of the frequent breakdowns and the rising outdoor temperatures.

After I complained repeatedly over a one month period, they reluctantly agreed to the installation of a complete new system. Within a few days, they had completed the unit installation and we were once again living in air conditioned comfort. I had my fingers crossed. In the meantime, they had changed the name of their company. This would raise eyebrows in any line of business, but i'm sure it is commonplace in Florida.

In order to keep the warranty active, I was obliged to have a system check after a six month break in period. When the technician arrived, he was a friendly fellow and gifted in the art of conversation. He noticed an autographed photo of a heavyweight boxer on my wall and told me he was at one time a boxer. A real overly friendly fellow. He was performing his diagnostic tests on the unit, going in and out of the house while engaging me in friendly conversation. At the conclusion of his testing, he told me that I needed additional work done on my air conditioning system that would be quite costly. His demeanor suddenly changed from the friendly down home guy that he was portraying to being strictly business. He was honing in for the kill!! He informed me that not only did I need to install a "biologic in duct air purifier", but that the duct work servicing the old system was not adequate to handle the air flow produced by the new system that they had just installed. (They conveniently neglected to inform me that the biologic system they would install would operate using a system of neon bulbs that would require replacement about once a year at the cost of about one hundred sixty dollars a bulb)

When he gave me the estimate for the upgrades, I was speechless. He quoted me a price of three thousand two hundred dollars for the biologic purifier system and and an additional cost of nine thousand dollars for the replacement of the duct work. (Visions of Jesse James quickly crossed my mind). He started what seemed to be a rehearsed spiel about the health problems that we could experience if we didn't install the system. (Although we had done very well for ten years without one) Then he contacted his supervisor who chimed in and quickly got my wife alarmed about the scourge of dust mites entering our home which quickly hit a nerve with her. He and his co-hort were addressing this like a life or death situation. I reluctantly agreed to install the unit at a forty percent discount. The technician's face lit up like he won the lotto and he quickly started the installation. ((I'm sure he was counting up his commission for this bit of salesmanship) I told them that I would be consulting a second a/c contractor for a second opinion and that the issue of replacing the duct work would be considered.

The next day, I contacted a second a/c company and told them what had transpired. He inspected the a/c system and told me that not only had I been grossly overcharged for the biologic system that was installed (even at forty percent off the quoted price), but a simple adjustment to the blower motor output would negate the need for new duct work. Now I was really fuming!!

I contacted the company who installed the system the next day and told them that if they did not refund a portion of my check I issued in the amount of one thousand nine hundred twenty dollars, I would file a complaint not only with the better business bureau, but I would also contact the attorney generals office. At first, they balked, but agreed after I divulged the source of my second opinion. I never had anything to do with the company after that and I'm sure they have gone through a few more name changes since then.

I do not mean to smear the many craftsman who operate in the state, I only want to forewarn residents that it is always smart to investigate any contractor who you hire to do work for you. Most of them are hardworking, honest people who will always treat their customers fairly and do quality work. There are a few though, that have no scruples and no qualms about not providing the service they are being paid for. They have always been around and always will be. CAVEOT EMPTOR!!

Richard T Vogt

34—FLORIDA LIVING

November 30, 2013

When I decided to make a permanent move to Florida with my wife, we had to decide just what type of of housing we wanted. There was not only the type of house to be considered but in what kind of environment the house would be situated. There are many choices in Florida. A house can be purchased in a gated community with a long list of rules and restrictions that must be obeyed. There are open community's that are not gated, but have the same requirements that some would feel are an infringement on personal libertys. A home can be purchased in a residential community with no restrictions at all. Trailer parks, towne homes, and condominiums can all be purchased with or without restrictions and rules. Many home buyers purchase a home in a deed restricted subdivision only to find after a short time that the rules are too stringent for them to adhere to. Restrictions such as no trucks allowed parked in the driveway, no swing sets in the yards, no statuary on the property, no basketball nets in the driveway, and no bird baths or feeders on the property. The list goes on and on. Permission must be granted in order to paint a house, and only in select colors. Want to paint your front door? Sorry, you have to get permission before the first brush stroke. Oops! You planted that bush and didn't get permission? Remove it! Disobey the rules and you will be subject to a fine which could be substantial.

These rules and restrictions are strictly enforced not only to create a clean orderly community, but to maintain property values for the homeowners. I don't mind the deed restrictions, but I have friends who wouldn't even consider moving to a community where such conditions are in effect. Its the old "free country" mindset and it is normal for some to feel that way. Most deed restricted subdivisions have beautiful landscaping which is maintained to Disneyland standards. Lakes and nature preserves abound which creates a haven for wildlife. But Home Owners Associations have a stigma attached to them and many potential home buyers will avoid homes located where there is an H.O.A.

There are about five hundred homes in the subdivision where I reside which is comprised of many different types of housing. I purchased a home with a "maintenance free" feature included in the deed. This means that I pay a quarterly fee to have a professional landscaper maintain my property. There are forty four homes in the section which are of three different types of architecture. The styles are intermingled so that the neighborhood doesn't have that "Levittown" appearance. My house is located in the Villa section. There are three other sections in the subdivision: Patio homes, cottage homes and estate homes. Each section is governed by a board of directors who are elected by the homeowners. There is a community board that has jurisdiction over not only the estate homes, but also the entire subdivision. This is known as a Home Owners Association or H.O.A. Getting confused? Wait! I'm just getting started. There is an architectural review committee which is appointed by the community board to review any changes to be made by property owners on their property. This applies to not only landscaping but to any changes to the outside of the home There is a pool committee responsible for the pool and its environs. There is a landscaping committee who oversees the grounds maintenance and the ponds within the entire subdivision.

The people who get elected to the board are from varied backgrounds. Some are genuinely interested in providing proper management for the community and there are some who are just interested in leaving their mark. A few have been elected only to be pushed aside by other board members because of a dispute on matters of policy. Some residents even campaign door to door to get elected. Meetings are held periodically which are open to homeowners where they are allowed to speak and participate.

When I first moved in my subdivision, there was a problem with unleashed dogs. The board in power at the time refused to do anything about it so I had a summons issued to a homeowner that was violating the leash law. That resulted in my being issued numerous summon's to appear in court to testify as a witness for the county. In the end, the case was dismissed because the judge ruled that the violation did not occur on county property but on private land. Well, I lost the battle but I won the war. When the residents elected a new board, they could envision the hazard that loose dogs presented to wildlife on the site and soon tired of phone calls from residents complaining about people not picking up the droppings from roaming dogs. The leash rule was given top priority, and enforced.

I moved to Florida to escape high taxes and the cold weather up in New York. Other than that, I wouldn't call Florida a "Paradise". During the winter tourist season, the heavy traffic has to be considered whenever a local trip is planned. It's an elderly population with elderly driving skills. The real estate brochures always show a nifty house with a pool in back all covered with a cage to keep out the bugs. But in reality, the water in the pools is usually too warm in the summer and really too cold during the winter. The heat in the summer is excruciating. When you walk out of an air conditioned enclosure, it feels like a blast furnace. Can you fry an egg on the sidewalk? Maybe! But the shrubbery thrives here in all this sand. I cant understand how they grow anything, it's just a big sand bar! If you are a beach bum or just like to deep fry your body, this is the place for you. It's one big beach. Ocean or Gulf, take your choice.

But there is a flip side to all this. Tennis anyone? Outdoor recreation never stops. If you can do it in the summer, you can do it in the winter. It's a golfers paradise here when they are chipping ice off their windshields up north. The rates go up, but what the heck, its only money! Flowers are in bloom everywhere you look. The blossoming bougainvillea in is breathtaking. Migrating waterfowl return and populate the marshlands. Four foot tall red headed sand hill cranes with six foot wingspans walk the streets like they own them. Great herons, bald eagles, and ducks of all types just waiting to be captured on film.

There is no need to hibernate, a long sleeved shirt will do it. Hurricanes aren't as prevalent as the news media make it seem. I have a neighbor who has lived in the area for fifty years and has never experienced a big blow. Property taxes can almost be paid out of petty cash if you don't have a champagne taste. Stick a heater in your pool and you can flop around like an Orca all winter. If you are into funky, head down to Key West. Anything goes in the Keys. If you are a Micky Mouse fan, Walt has amusements in Orlando that will keep you busy all season. (But bring your checkbook).

I was surprised at the number of elderly people living in the area when I moved down here. And because of that, the young people tend to move away when they finish their education. I think that the west coast of Florida attracts more seniors than the east coast. The west coast is more laid back and is geared more to senior living. Go to any large gathering here and it is always a sea of gray hair. When I go to church, I don't see anyone under fifty years old. I often wonder how the religious organizations will perpetuate their missions in the future. I guess the young people will grow into it as they get closer to the finish line and get a little nervous.

Dining out in Florida usually involves an early bird special or a coupon. Many senior citizens don't have very good night vision and want to get home before the sun sets. Restaurants open their doors at about four in the afternoon and many close the doors at nine in the evening. There are restaurants galore in the area serving just about any kind of food a diner would desire. Despite the abundance of eating establishments ready to serve the public, if you dont arrive by five thirty, you will have a long wait before you put on a bib. Eating out is a form of recreation here in sunny Florida that people compare to going to see a play. It is interesting to see how many couples dine alone. I always thought that it showed that they were either very much in love or just tired of the blather of of other people.

After all is said and done, I would say that Florida is worth a shot. After the mortgage is paid off, the kids have flown the coop, and you can't stay warm in winter no matter how hard you try, C'mon down and give it a test drive. It's not for everybody, but it just might be for you!

Richard (Digger) Vogt

35—RHINE RIVER CRUISE

November 16, 2013

"True all inclusive luxury European river cruise. The worlds only authentic botique cruise line" The advertisement looked inviting. Probing further into their brochure, I found a cruise down the Rhine river. My wife and I were both of German ancestry and had always had a desire to visit "the Fatherland". We both went to a travel agency to investigate the possibility of taking one of their advertised cruises. The initial dates we had planned were booked solid so we had to find a new date that would coincide with my wife's schedule at the hospital. The agent made the cruise sound more exiting and pleasurable based on her having completed the same cruise we were contemplating two months previously. We discussed the fact that we would need a passport and were told the agency would take the photos necessary free of charge. The agent then explained the various accommodations that were available on the boat and any additional charges that we could expect from various shore excursions that would be included in the itinerary. Dress codes were discussed as was the policy of the cruise line to accommodate special dietary needs. (We were both vegetarians) The prices for various types of staterooms were discussed and we selected accommodations that were within the range of what we had budgeted for.

Neither of us were what I would call seasoned travelers and considering the lengthy flight we would have from the U S A to Europe, we decided to fly first class. Thats when we discovered that luxury really does cost money. We had our passport photos taken (they were scary), got our passports, and we were ready to" fly the friendly sky". It was about then that reality started to sink in and I realized what I had just committed to. Now, as I mentioned previously, I am not a seasoned traveler, therefore, when I go on any trip that requires lengthy travel, I am assaulted with a bout of anxiety. We had a few weeks to wait before the departure date so I figured it would pass. But no, It hung on like a rock star groupie. Along with the anxiety, there is an added feature which I shall describe as "the trots" which required keeping lavatory services close at hand. But thats not all. Along with the trots comes what the old genteel southern ladies used to call the "vapors". Now that can be deadly!

I knew that my wife had her heart set on not only on visiting Duetchland. but also enjoying that cruise down the "Romantic Rhine". So when the departure date arrived I stocked up on kaopectate and off we went. The first sign of trouble came when the boarding agent at the Tampa airport red flagged a small souvenir pocket knife I had attatched to my key chain. I was told I would either have to surrender the one and one half inch knife or go back to the main terminal and mail it back to myself at home. Back on the shuttle I go to mail my "weapon" home. Our departure from Tampa to Newark N J was delayed and despite the boarding agent assuring us we would have "plenty of time between flights" we arrived in Newark with about ten minutes to our next flight. Despite running at breakneck speed to the next flight, the door was closed when we got there. That flight would have taken us directly to Amsterdam where we would board our cruise boat. Now we had to negotiate a new flight. We caught a ride on a 777 going to Heathrow in the U K. That is quite an airplane. A sleeper with a gourmet meal served at eleven o'clock in the evening. Now, already running late, we had a layover in Heathrow. I will say that the waiting room for first class passengers looked like it was designed by the Donald himself.

A short hop, and we were in Amsterdam. Now, there is a wacky city. Canibis for breakfast, lunch and dinner. A guy pedaling a mobile bar down the street with four guys on stools getting sloshed at two in the afternoon. Departure time for our boat was at two in the afternoon. We arrived at three o'clock in the afternoon. When we went to pick up our luggage, it never arrived. I decided that I would leave the terminal to try and locate a cruise line agent while my wife filed a claim for our luggage. I was told by security that once I left the terminal, I couldn't return, but locating a cruise line agent was crucial. I left the terminal with much trepidation. Luckily, there was an agent a few steps from the exit door and he assured me that he would get us on the boat. I couldn't communicate in any way with my wife inside the terminal and on top of that, she had my passport. The agent told me to go to the travelers aid station and ask them to make an announcement inside the terminal asking my wife to come out. (while all this is going on, the kaopectate just aint working)! My wife finally came out sans luggage and the agent put us into a taxi for a ride to the dock where we would board a very large bus for a trip to the next town to connect with the boat. By now, we hadn't showered in twenty four hours. (Although in Europe that wouldn't even be close to a record).

We boarded the large tour bus and were transported to a town about twenty five miles down the river. The ride was actually an added feature to our trip. We got to see the little picturesque villages close up and watch the townspeople busy with their daily routines. We waited, and we waited, and we waited. Then the bow of the boat came into view on the crowded Rhine river. We were waiting by a sea wall where the boat would dock to pick us up. It was a long boat and I doubted if the captain could bring the vessel in that close. But he executed a skillful maneuver and we were welcomed on board. We were never so glad to jump into a shower. We had no fresh clothes but we were afloat at last. Our luggage was finally retrieved by the concierge three days after boarding. Luckily my wife had packed a travel bag which we carried on the plane that saved the day.

I was surprised at the rapid flow of the river and the number of barges using it as a seagoing highway. A barge on the Rhine is home to the family working it. They have their auto on board and have a crane lift it off when they tie up in a town. Barges are used to carry all sorts of commodities. We went through six locks where the boat was lowered each time to accommodate the terrain. The scenery along the river was out of a storybook. Quaint little villages nestled in the mountains, castles high up on the hill, abandoned towers close to the shore that were used to collect tolls centurys ago when the church ruled the waterway. There is a one hundred mile stretch of the river where no bridges are allowed. Sheep graze on the rolling hills along the banks and that is their only purpose, to keep the shoreline looking like a fresh military haircut. There are acres and acres of vineyards along the banks with the rows of vines set out with proper European precision. Cathedrals and churches abound in the villages and can be identified by their majestic spires towering over the landscape. Every turn in the river brought a new vista to behold.

The accommodations were first class as was the food. It was an open dining plan which provided an opportunity to meet other interesting people. Every evening after dinner we were entertained by various musical groups that were professional in every way. We stopped in a different town every day and were either offered guided tours or were free to wander about on our own. In France, we had a female tour guide with an attitude that reeked of Parisian arrogance. At one point in the tour, someone in the group attempted to take a photo of her and she shrieked," no! no! no!, you do not take my peekchure without you first ask me!" Her outlandish colors that really clashed made her look like something out of Alice in Wonderland (umbrella and all). Wandering around the towns and cities made me realize that even though the buildings were older, people are people wherever you go. We visited a winery where a few people made fools out of themselves and a cuckoo clock factory where an oriental passenger from Hong Kong purchased an elaborate clock for the princely price of fifteen hundred dollars. We visited a centuries old castle and had to climb a hill so steep, I didn't think I was going to make it only to find that we had eighteen more steep stairs awaiting us. The cruise terminated in Basil Switzerland where the airport had soldiers patrolling the terminal with sub machine guns. Then on to Frankfort Germany where black clad policeman patrolled using sedgeway people movers. Then on to the good old U S of A. It was a nice trip that I will always remember, just me, my loving wife and my bottle of kaopectate.

Richard T Vogt

ABOUT THE AUTHOR

Richard T. Vogt was born in the city of Peekskill New York in 1932 and lived in a section of the city known as "Finktown" where he aquired the nickname of "Digger" from one of the older boys. He graduated from Peekskill High School and Joined the U.S. Navy during the Korean War and traveled the world over during his four year enlistment. He married and had three children. He was employed by a large computer company for thirty four years. A musician, Digger has played with many dance bands and drum corps in the Hudson Valley for 30 years. He got divorced after 19 years of marriage then got remarried a second time and has been married for 36 years to his second wife Marlene. In addition to three children, he has four grandchildren and one great grandchild.